YOU ARE CORDIALLY INVITED TO

THE WEDDING MARCH

A TRUE STORY

Rob Smat

YOU ARE CORDIALLY INVITED TO

THE WEDDING MARCH

A TRUE STORY

GAUDIUM

Gaudium Publishing

Las Vegas ◊ Chicago ◊ Palm Beach

Published in the United States of America by
Histria Books
7181 N. Hualapai Way, Ste. 130-86
Las Vegas, NV 89166 U.S.A
HistriaBooks.com

Gaudium Publishing is an imprint of Histria Books. Titles published under the imprints of Histria Books are distributed worldwide.

Library of Congress Control Number: 2023948274

ISBN 978-1-59211-382-8 (hardcover)
ISBN 978-1-59211-403-0 (eBook)

CONTENTS

For Kate, the loveliest

AUTHOR'S NOTE

How does one write about the first global pandemic in a century, and one that brought our nation's social fabric to its knees on more than one occasion? Moreover, how does one talk about the gray areas of something like COVID?

This was a pandemic that lasted weeks, months, or until the federal emergency officially ended on May 11th, 2023, according to who you ask. I couldn't possibly encompass its breadth. The magnitude of the saga will be studied in the years, and by the generations, still to come.

What I do know is someone needed to tell Amy's story, and her story was intrinsically connected with almost every part of the COVID era.

For that reason, I like to think of this book as the story of COVID, as many of us experienced it: one day at a time.

The Wedding March started as a documentary script. Then, that outline became a long-form piece of journalistic writing. But nonfiction writing requires facts—and more importantly—answers. In the era of COVID, no one had the answers. Even truth was eroded to the point of personal opinion, something which every public figure, private citizen, and political party was guilty of.

As a result, Amy's story deserved a narrativized approach, albeit one that relies on the most factual of reports, footage, and social media posts.

So this isn't a made-up story, or one that's excessively glamorized. It's an account. It's an account that preserves the best and worst moments of a unique moment in American history, and one whose details have been frequently overwritten, forgotten, or erased altogether.

This book is anchored to true events. It reflects the subjects' present recollections of experiences over time. Some names and characteristics have been changed, some events have been compressed, and some dialogue has been recreated.

Chapters recounted in the first person are from my own recollections and records from this winding tale. And the Judge Judy episode details have been reconstructed from memory rather than a transcript.

As I started work on this manuscript, around the time when the masks on planes had started to come off, kids had returned to school across the country, and inflation had begun its steady climb toward the heavens, a friend of mine responded to my topic with curiosity.

"A wedding planner during COVID? That's a tough one, because her entire job would be the source of super-spreader events."

That statement stuck with me. Just like the truth during COVID, that notion was accurate, until it wasn't. And that point in time differed, depending on who you asked.

Heroes and villains of this book, myself included, will be defined by where a reader believes such a line belongs. The principal complaint belonging to this book's protagonists, though, is that the real-life events lacked such demarcations. When CAPE begged for resolution of the gray areas, they were only dealt more infuriating ambiguity.

When governments—local, state, or federal—cracked down on pandemic activities, the prison yard spotlight only seemed to shine on those who abided by the law, or the industries that were politically advantageous to mandate. Even those state or local governments most focused on equity seemed to act with extreme prejudice when the tides of politics demanded such.

If there's one thing we can all agree on, it's that no person or policy was perfect from beginning to end of COVID. For that, we might all wish to collectively forget the time.

But Amy's story shouldn't be forgotten.

To paraphrase a meaningful piece of insight from one of my interviewees: COVID deserves a detailed after-action report, and one that's focused on evils of omission, rather than pointing fingers at perceived commissions.

Finally, as George Santayana famously said, "Those who cannot remember the past are condemned to repeat it."

1
WELLNESS CHECK

San Diego, CA – 8:30 p.m., Jan. 26th, 2021

Amy Ulkutekin had received plenty of stressful emails in her time as a wedding coordinator, event planner, and entrepreneur, but she'd never been so distraught after sending one.

She had spent the last few hours struggling to dissipate the residual adrenaline still coursing through her veins. While a nice bath might have calmed her down, Amy wasn't the type to sit still. At least not when she, her husband, and two children needed laundry done.

As any entrepreneur knows, no amount of business success or failure takes priority over family. And tonight, the family needed the laundry done.

Amy had always felt like a shark in her combined role as a wedding planner, event planner, and small business owner: if she stopped swimming, she might as well stop breathing too. Nonetheless, her "ocean" had felt smaller with each passing day of the COVID pandemic, and soon, there wouldn't be any ocean left.

That's what she'd attempted to explain in her email, anyway, addressed to the administrative members of the California governorship.

But that was the past now. Tonight, Amy would continue folding T-Rex pajamas, ragged college t-shirts, and the occasional unmatched sock.

Almost on cue, and just as she was getting into the rhythm of chores, Amy's son, E.J., was beckoning from downstairs in that demanding way that children never quite realize feels callous.

"Moooom?"

E.J. and Amy's daughter Ariana were a year apart, and still in those childhood years that made them resilient, ebullient, and adorable in the way that they would inevitably lose as pre-teens. The pandemic had been tough for them, especially in the early days when parks and schools were closed. And they weren't out of it yet, even if the latest pandemic threats were no longer boredom or death, but the family's dwindling finances.

It didn't take long for Amy to put two-and-two together as to why E.J. had been calling for her. There was a firm knocking from their front door, which was never a good sign so late into the evening.

Once or twice, Amy was used to receiving a last-minute delivery of wedding materials before a couple's big day, but there wouldn't be any weddings in the foreseeable future.

Amy left the pile of clothes in the bedroom and made her way to the top of the stairs, looking down into the living room.

"How are you feeling, E.J.?"

E.J.'s health was still top of mind for her, placed in that part of her brain where she was ready for anything that could suddenly take a turn for the worse. Less than a week ago, E.J. had been diagnosed with type 1 diabetes, and fully hospitalized for diabetic ketoacidosis. While the Ulkutekins were lucky to escape tragedy, E.J.'s five-day hospital stay felt like a straw that could break the camel's back.

"Good, Mom."

"Let me know if not," Amy offered, as she descended the stairs, her mind already shifting to the red and blue lights flooding through their windows.

Police cruisers covered the usually mundane neighborhood street outside.

"I wasn't sure if I should open the door. You said—"

"You did good, hon."

"You said to trust the police, but not strangers, and that police officer looked like a stranger—"

"You did good. Thanks kiddo."

E.J. pursed his lips, nodded, and turned back to watching the TV.

Amy's pulse rose as she neared the door, in a very similar way to when her heart raced with red and blue lights in the rearview mirror on the 805. At least when that was the case, you knew it was about a speeding ticket or a busted taillight. This could be anything.

At least it wasn't something horrible about the kids or her husband, who she knew to be inside the house. That kept her panic at bay for the time being.

When she opened the door, two officers, a man and a woman, stood on her front doorstep, right next to a Prime package she hadn't realized had been delivered earlier that day.

Amy smiled politely, squinting as the flashing lights flooded her sight.

"Hi. Is everything alright?"

She noticed their demeanors shift ever so slightly, as if they had prepared to be greeted by a shotgun-wielding maniac and could relax.

"Are you Amy Ulk—"

She interrupted, helping with the tough pronunciation.

"Ulkutekin?"

That last name had always been a mouthful.

"Yes, right," the male officer corrected himself.

"That's me."

He nodded.

"We're here to make a wellness check."

Their badges were easier to read as Amy's eyes adjusted to the dark. Under their last names were patches that read SUICIDE PREVENTION.

If Amy thought her stress levels were elevated earlier that day, this was her new record. She didn't know her heart could beat so fast.

"I'm not suicidal."

"Good."

"What's going on?"

The female officer specified, "The governor's office was concerned, after an email they'd received from you."

Amy's jaw dropped in disbelief, especially as she got a better look at the extent of public resources that had been dispatched to her front yard. Her email requesting an audience with California's public health leaders had merited no less than eight officers and three squad cars.

Amy's voice caught in her throat as she became increasingly self-aware of every detail of her being.

"I just... I just wanted a meeting with them."

The confusion only intensified from there. It would be minutes before Amy would return indoors.

E.J. was quick when she got there.

"What did they want?"

Mystified, Amy could only utter, "They said it's about Newsom."

It wasn't the first time in the past year that E.J. or Ariana had looked at Amy sideways. Whether it was her transformation into an activist, part-time state lobbyist, or even as a contestant on Judge Judy, Amy had become a whole new person in just ten short months, and her family struggled to keep up.

It wasn't the cops that surprised them most that year, though. It was the day Amy buttoned her family up in tuxedos and wedding dresses and marched through the streets of Sacramento with hundreds of other protestors, all dressed for the weddings they could no longer celebrate.

2
HEAD START

Eighty-two.

It was a number Amy never thought she'd see, but it was staring her right in the face, at the top of her annual events spreadsheet.

Eighty-two weddings to plan, coordinate, and orchestrate during the year 2020. The number was mind boggling, even with the two or three Amy had accomplished in the first weeks of the calendar year.

Amy's company, First Comes Love, had planned maybe sixty-five weddings in the busiest year leading up to this one. Eighty-two was a behemoth by comparison. It thrilled Amy just as much as it gave her a nervous electricity.

That's not to say Amy didn't have a pot of gold at the end of this rainbow: she was going to upgrade from her Toyota to a Tesla, her dream car.

While her RAV4 was easier to navigate with her taller-than-average height (which yes, came very much in handy keeping track of people during events), it was the Tesla that would bring her all the modern conveniences she'd so desired, with a slight hit to leg room.

With a home office that faced the street outside her house, it was an hourly occurrence to have one of those zero emission, carpool lane-accessible, technological wonders silently glide past the window. Or speed past, well above the limit. Her eyes would draw away from her work for only a moment before refocusing, fearing that any loss of focus might unravel her chance to reach that battery-powered light at the end of the tunnel.

The year 2020 was the culmination of a decade of Amy's life, and it was too perfect that her line of work would intersect with a year so prosperous for couples around the world, many of whom hoped to marry in her backyard of San Diego.

The breakneck pace of Amy's current situation made her think back on past times, during which she'd yearned for such prosperity. Before being a wedding planner, Amy was a corporate events planner. But one usually followed the other. Weddings were just more intimate events, with one to five hundred of your closest friends and family members.

That wasn't part of the plan when Amy left her first job out of college to work at Fleishman Hillard's Southern California office. The corporate event space made a great beginning for Amy, but it was just that: corporate. With the experience Amy had gained from planning for Virgin Airlines, Qantas, and the opening of a Las Vegas hotel or two, she was ready to sink her teeth into an industry where she could pave her own path, and one where she could form more personal connections.

All it took was a financial crisis to get her there, and not the one that loomed a few weeks down the road.

While life got busy, it never got so busy that Amy didn't think back on that cloudy day back in 2008 when the regional manager at Fleishman had come down from the San Francisco office. In any recession, it's events and tourism that hurt first, and as soon as the bigwig stepped off the elevator, Amy knew the end was finally here.

After a day of watching her peers, friends, and even a mentor or two make their way from desk to the conference room and back, totally stripped of everything they'd worked for, Amy was called up for her execution.

Her mind had been swirling with what she would do next, and how she could possibly land on her feet, especially as the slowdown only seemed to be starting. The dizzying confusion of losing one's 9-to-5 gave way to the hungry determination to survive. It was in that moment that Amy realized a need to chase her passion.

Weddings were recession-proof. Even at smaller scales, no one stopped getting married just because times got tough. That would bring her comfort, seeing how well things had gone for other industries at this moment in time.

"Amy? We're ready for you," her manager said grimly, turning back to the conference room, metaphorically caked with the blood of her co-workers' careers.

Once in the room, she sat down across from the manager, someone from human resources, and the San Francisco bigwig, but she wasn't afraid after all she'd done to brace herself that day. Amy knew she would throw everything she had at a meaningful pivot the minute the first severance check arrived.

"You know, Amy," her manager started, "We value you quite a bit around here. As you know, we're having to make some difficult decisions in light of what's happening. We're happy to say the company's going to be OK. But we still need to downsize, all the same."

Enough with the fluff, Amy had thought. Just bring down the hammer and let's stop delaying the inevitable. Wasting time was never Amy's strong suit. In event planning, time is more than just money. Time is everything.

"We'd like you to join our New York office. We'll be closing a few, including this one, to bring all our resources together."

Had Amy feared firing, this might have made her jaw drop to the floor in joy, but instead she only felt conflicted as her manager untied the noose and allowed her to step off the proverbial gallows.

"You're not firing me?"

The bigwig shook her head and piped in, "We'd just need you to move to the East Coast. Probably time for it, considering the San Diego office only had so many projects. We absolutely see a future with you at the company."

Amy sighed as her manager suggested, "If you'd like some time to consider—"

"I'm staying in San Diego," she blurted out.

It might have seemed like a gut decision, but this was well thought out by now. Maybe if they'd started with her earlier that morning, she'd have taken the time, or moved to New York. But now, she was sure.

"Thank you, for everything."

Before they knew what hit them, Amy was back out the door again, a new lease on life, spurred by what felt like a near-death experience.

There wasn't much at her desk worth boxing up, but she didn't have time to start the task before her friend and mentor, Steph, walked over from her office.

"Amy, I'm so sorry. I fought for you to stay on. I thought—"

Amy cut her short.

"It worked! They didn't fire me."

"Oh gosh. I could have sworn you were over here packing up your things."

"I am," Amy chuckled.

Steph tilted her head, not computing.

"I'm going to start my own company. It's something I've needed for a long time. Just didn't realize until now."

Steph nodded.

"Seems like your mind's made up."

Amy nodded.

"You've got a great future ahead of you, Amy."

She smiled warmly and gave Amy a hug.

That had stuck with Amy ever since Steph had said it and meant more to her than any employee-of-the-month or bonus had.

Eighty-two weddings would put a smile on Steph's face a decade later, no doubt. Amy had fulfilled the prophecy.

As any wedding planner would do, Amy made the best of the available circumstances in 2009. She founded First Comes Love within the year. She serviced friends she knew who were getting married, and then ramped up production with staff members, great word-of-mouth, and a rapidly expanding network of clients across the West Coast.

Within a year or two, First Comes Love had already topped fifty weddings, and it didn't slow down one bit after that.

In the years that followed, Amy would establish two more small businesses, Catalyst Creative and the Best Coast Beer Festival, both of which were also successes. Best Coast's fifth annual festival would be on March 21st, 2020, and had provided Amy a welcome annual reprieve from weddings, especially during the slower months of February and March.

Still staring at the tally at the top of her spreadsheet, Amy appreciated a still moment to reflect before her next call, which wasn't with a couple or a vendor, but instead would be a member of San Diego's tourism office, Paula.

Thanks to the Best Coast Fest, Amy had formed great connections with city leadership in a way that weddings alone would never have provided. Though, she didn't think that was ever terribly important outside of grants or funding.

Until today, that is.

By now Amy had seen the World Health Organization's warnings about the novel coronavirus, which caused stocks to dip by a good amount the day prior, and still seemed to have the world on edge. She wasn't worried about stocks so much as her stock of Best Coast Festival merchandise, which was currently in her garage. The merch cost her over a hundred grand and was one of many investments she'd hoped to turn to profit in the week to come.

It was her due diligence to reach out to Paula and at least get a scoop from inside city hall, hoping for the best, and being prepared for whatever else might be in store. If there was increased testing, Amy wanted a head start on getting those swabs. If it was temperature checks, she would visit every superstore and pharmacy across America's most populous state, looking for thermometers.

Whatever it took, Amy could usually pull it off, especially with a head start. The best events are all about having a head start.

At last, the silence of Amy's electric car daydreams, flashbacks to 2008, and anticipation of a monstrous year ahead were broken by the ringing of her iPhone, which she answered.

"This is Amy."

"Hi Amy, I've got Paula for you when you're ready."

"Thanks."

Because multitasking usually resulted in missed details, Amy made it a point to almost never multitask during a call. But there was no temptation to worry about the eighty-two vertical cells any longer than she already had. She waited, ready to transcribe anything and everything Paula might have to say, and then multiply that by however many weddings she had for the month immediately following Best Coast.

The line clicked, and Paula was on.

"Hello, Amy."

She sounded stressed. Paula was big in the tourism department, and while that gave her plenty of tough choices, she usually handled even the toughest of crises with a great poker face.

Hello wasn't a great poker face.

"Hi Paula! Thanks for making time for me. Hope you're doing well."

"I figured you'd be calling," she sighed, like someone whose kid had accidentally dinged your car in a parking lot and had left a note.

Paula had only helped Amy over the years, and she'd been especially vital for this year's Best Coast festival. So why she sounded like this, Amy wasn't sure.

"Oh, really?"

Paula groaned, "It's all such a mess so far. I can't even begin to tell you."

"I saw the CROSS'd Fest went forward," Amy offered.

"CROSS'd? Uh, we're not so sure."

Amy hadn't been concerned before this moment, but Paula's silence changed that.

"I've got my pen out, ready to take down what you think. Started reaching out to some connections I might have to get some thermometers—"

"Amy, what do you know?"

Amy disliked plenty of things. But ignorance was at the top of that list.

"About what?"

"In a few days, the mayor's office is going to announce stay-at-home orders."

The words hit her like a truck.

Stay-at-home. No amount of event wizardry could top stay-at-home.

What a stupid public relations version of "quarantine" that was. It was a quarantine without the teeth to enforce it.

Paula concluded, "For now, we're done."

Amy felt a pit open in her stomach. If her mind had been anywhere else in that moment, it was now wholly focused on Paula's every word, with the occasional thought toward the hundred thousand dollars of cotton, polyester, and neon plastic now sitting worthless in her garage.

Nonetheless, Amy was a cool operator. Where others go through the stages of grief when they get terrible news, Amy didn't. No event planner worth their salt has the time for denial, anger, bargaining, and depression when acceptance is the quickest way to a meaningful solution.

"Oh wow."

That was all she could muster.

Paula relaxed a bit, especially since Amy hadn't launched into the expletive-laced tirade Paula might have feared.

"All I can say is, you need to prepare."

"OK. I will."

That was all she could say before hanging up.

Moments later, Amy would regret not thanking Paula for letting her in on the news, but it seemed that Amy's levelheadedness was thanks enough for Paula, who had likely had some more contentious conversations, and would face many more when the news came out.

"Damn it."

She had 48 hours at most and would use up every minute of that until San Diego mayor Kevin Faulconer stepped behind his podium to break the news to the unsuspecting public.

Even with the six figures of hats, tees, and frisbees in her garage, Amy's priority was her clients. She zoomed to the top of the eighty-two cells and picked out an immediate handful. Three rapidly fired calls merited three blissfully ignorant bubbly voicemails from her brides-to-be.

"Hiii, this is Brittany. Can't get to the phone right now, but–"

BEEP.

"This is Amy. Call me as soon as you get this."

So much for the gradual rise in weddings leading up to the busy summer. It was DEFCON 1 as Amy scrambled to list May, June, and July venues that would accept her March and April couples in a worst-case scenario. After that, it was listing vendors to contact to check for later summer availability, which was highly unlikely, though some would undoubtedly work miracles.

"Hi, this is Amy with the April eleventh wedding. I'd like to see what the venue's availability looks like later in the summer, just in case there's some change in the next four weeks with the coronavirus. Thank you."

Beep.

Some vendors she got on the phone and others she left messages for. The ones she spoke to all had the same response.

"Uh, I'm sure we could figure it out."

"We don't see any reason to worry right now."

"We're happy to do whatever you'd like, but don't think it'll come to that."

It was the lack of worry that troubled Amy most.

There wouldn't be time for sleep later that evening, but she did have an hour or two before vendors and brides would start replying to her messages and calls. That would be her only chance to prepare her own family for a potential societal fallout. It's not like anyone knew what was going to happen, anyway.

Amy tried to keep her concerns about the Best Coast Festival at bay as she peeled out of the driveway in her RAV4, knowing that there would be a need for a larger conversation with the festival staff, which she would urgently schedule for the next morning, if not that evening. The Skype invite was already en route.

As if the sky-high shelves full of pallets of wholesale goods lit by skylights wasn't bizarre enough, the familiar Chula Vista Costco felt even more dystopian that

Monday afternoon as Amy flashed her membership card to the grinning greeter at the front door.

No one in this building would have a grin on their faces another week from now as people started violently amassing dry goods, canned foods, and hand sanitizer.

Rushing past San Diegans casually browsing corporate clothing, airline gift cards, and party dinnerware, it was blatantly obvious that no one else had any clue. Amy wanted to warn them, climb up on the tallest platform of Sue Grisham books in the center of the superstore, and shout like Cassandra to the ancient Trojans.

The world as you know it is coming to an end! Don sackcloth and pray for mercy!

Her phone rang with the first of her brides returning her initial call. She could multitask now. This wouldn't be the first call she'd taken at a wholesale club, anyway.

Amy pulled the comically wide shopping cart into an aisle full of chairs and folding tables, a part of the store she'd frequented before many an event.

"Hello!"

"Hi, Amy! Sorry I missed you!"

"No, no that's alright."

This call was from Savannah, who'd interned with Amy for eight months during the year prior. Amy liked Savannah, and she'd considered hiring her to First Comes Love when she was out of school. But instead, Savannah had asked Amy to marry her and her college sweetheart.

The ceremony would be in two weeks and would be held at the Don Room at the El Cortez. It was one of the weddings Amy was most excited about, yet now it posed the greatest dilemma.

"Is now good?" Savannah asked, knowing Amy's busy schedule firsthand.

"Yeah, I'll be quick."

Amy began filling a cart with dry goods, knowing she'd return to fill a second cart with perishables.

"Listen, I know you've probably been keeping an eye on the news," Amy began.

"Oh yeah. Always something."

"Well, that something's coming here."

"Here?"

"They're going to do a lockdown, here in San Diego."

"Like, for 'two weeks to flatten the curve?'"

"I think it will be long enough that I wanted you to know, so you can have a backup plan if you need one."

If Savannah had been Amy's client, she might have been firmer about the backup plan, but since she was only partially helping, and knew Savannah knew just as much as she did, Amy trusted she'd make the right choice.

But the right choice was taking more time than Amy expected, as Savannah stayed quiet on the other end of the phone.

"I think whatever happens, we're just going to show up and have the wedding."

Amy frowned.

"I don't think you will. The government will be saying you can't, and they've never done that for events. It's like that wedding at Scripps we had to redo. You only get one chance at getting vendors locked in for backup dates and—"

"It's just, yeah, Amy—"

"And you could end up throwing an event where there's a spread—"

"Yeah Amy, yeah yeah. It's just, we're just going to do it, and try not to worry about what happens."

And that was it. There wasn't any thought given beyond that. During this first and most potent strain of the disease, it was thinking like this that got people killed after events like this one, and not just the elderly or comorbid either.

Amy suspected as much but didn't have enough data to force the subject. No amount of case numbers from Italy, the most visible and transparent outbreak to date, would make a difference to Savannah.

Hanging up the phone after a cordial goodbye and repeated congratulations, Amy absolved herself of her guilt, at least for that couple. She was now a false prophet to both her clients and the unsuspecting Costco shoppers around her. They wouldn't believe her, and if they did, it wouldn't change them.

Amy didn't get any sideways looks as she checked out the first time, but when she came back with the second cart full of fridge and freezer goods, the checker gave her a sideways glance.

"Restocking your earthquake kit?" he asked.

"Yeah, and the big one's coming, in two days."

The checker grinned and chuckled, as did the receipt checker at the door, and E.J. too, when Amy would get home that night, futilely asking her children for help carrying the groceries inside.

The nonbelievers collectively stood in the shade of the giant wooden ark that Amy had just finished, not believing her warnings of great flood. But Amy wasn't a soothsayer, even if her preparedness had made her seem so later that month.

If she had been, she would have bought toilet paper.

There was no warning about that mad rush for toilet paper.

3
THE SUMMER WIND

Sacramento, CA – March 19th, 2020

There had never been this many eyes on one of Gavin Newsom's livestreams.

The California Governor's official Facebook page, where livestreams were broadcast, typically garnered a few thousand views per video, if even. In Gavin's entire tenure as San Francisco's mayor, those numbers had been even smaller.

Tonight, five times that many people were already tuned in. By the end of the broadcast, those view counts could very well top a quarter million. And for good reason. This announcement would change the way of life for a state, one which was larger than most countries.

In all fairness, updates on state incentives, homelessness initiatives, and tax law didn't interest the average person much more than they interested Gavin himself. But this wasn't day-to-day government. It was a quickly accelerating crisis.

Gavin's words would change everything, not just for Californians, but also the rest of the United States, because so many other governors and legislative bodies followed the Golden State's example.

Despite the once-in-a-lifetime challenge that he faced, the governor was uniquely positioned for what was on the horizon, thanks to a number of factors. For one, even though he'd only been California's governor for two years, a position formerly held by Jerry Brown and even Arnold Schwarzenegger before that, Gavin had been in public service ever since his appointment to the San Francisco Traffic Commission. That stint was followed by a role on the City Council, later becoming San Francisco's mayor, and finally followed by his lieutenant governorship under Gov. Brown.

While it was exciting to be climbing the ranks year after year, Gavin sensed that people in higher positions became increasingly insulated from the average citizen.

That's why he still rolled up his sleeves, given the opportunity, and wasn't afraid of the dirty work.

The opportunity to address Californians directly was just the kind of thing Gavin looked forward to.

With a front-row seat to Silicon Valley, his career had blossomed alongside the likes of Steve Jobs, Larry Ellison, and countless others. In the same way that these thinkers had innovated technology, Gavin hoped to innovate government, which he'd watched grow less innovative in the same span of time. That was the thesis of his book, Citizenville, anyway. And lines from his book still rang true in his present career.

"The biggest problem with government today is that we've set it up to manage problems, not solve them…. Too often, programs are just Band-Aids, not cures."

Gavin couldn't cure the novel coronavirus. He couldn't develop a vaccine any better than the federal government could. But he could solve problems, especially those wrought by the disease.

It was odd to think back on the title of his political thesis, a play on the once-popular FarmVille web game. Even the book's references to *Angry Birds* could be considered ancient history, only eight years after it was published by Penguin Books. But the core truths still held: in a world intrinsically united by smartphones, ubiquitous internet connectivity, and other devices, how had governments—at all levels—remained "dumb"?

Gavin hadn't expected his book to make waves outside of the governments he could personally influence, but he had hoped that someone would have picked up on his ideas by now, ideas that included a social media network for city and state leaders to share policy successes, a public/private partnership to fix potholes and litter akin to web games, or even something as simple as city-wide Wi-Fi. Unfortunately, few of those had come to fruition a decade later.

Citizenville continued to be a work in progress, and today would be his opportunity to embark on its next stage. It was times like these that people realized they didn't live in vacuums, that the government did in fact play an active—and inherently positive—role in their lives, as independent as they may think themselves to be.

"We experience government every single day, directly and indirectly. But because government can't brand all its projects with its own little Nike swoosh, people don't realize that fact. Because government doesn't have an official PR department to help burnish its image, people go about their daily lives oblivious to how enriched they are by it."

Gavin was the governor's PR department, and for once, the people were open to government working for them, something he'd desperately wished to see in his time as state leader.

Adlai Stevenson had said, "As citizens of this democracy, you are the rulers and the ruled, the law-givers and the law-abiding, the beginning and the end."

Once a diffused diaspora, this would be Californians' chance to come together to face down a common enemy.

Government 2.0 launched today, and the 250,000-odd viewers on Facebook would be the first to see it in action.

As Gavin reviewed his notes one final time, he watched as the public health leaders aligned behind his podium, where he'd approach as the stream kicked off. He always tried to time broadcasts that way, so people didn't just think of him as someone leading from behind a podium. He was a citizen just like everyone else, and that's something he'd carried with him since his days as a small business owner in San Francisco.

The feed went live, which Gavin could see on a screen to his left, where the governor's seal remained stagnant over a white background.

A woman in a headset stepped toward him from behind a control panel.

"We're ready when you are."

"Let's give it one more minute," he suggested.

She nodded.

"We'll go live with your go ahead, for the walkup."

"That's right."

The lights flashed red across the control center, which could be seen through the glass behind the podium, which itself had been lit up by a series of ceiling lights barely visible in the top edge of the framed shot.

The control room looked like it was ready for war, and one that could be shown, because the enemy was inanimate, and wouldn't gain an advantage seeing what the public health department knew about its increasing position.

It wasn't what the CDPH knew about COVID that worried Gavin, though. It was what they didn't. Thanks to severely limited testing and long turnaround times, they suspected COVID was already rapidly spreading across his state and had all but overrun the other coast of the country.

Unlike New York's Governor, Gavin wouldn't hesitate, especially with such a valuable head start. It was only that morning that the confusion in Cuomo's office had been apparent, which had been the talk of Gavin's staffers that morning, thanks to the latest episode of *The Daily*:

Producer: "If [CNN] says New York City tells 8 million people to be prepared to shelter in place, that is not going to happen?"

Cuomo: "No."

Producer: "But it's playing on the television right now."

Cuomo: "Yeah, I know. I know."

Producer: "What are you going to do?"

Cuomo: "Yeah, I don't know anyone at CNN. Yeah. But see how scary that is?"

Barbaro: "Your brother [Chris] is an anchor on CNN."

Cuomo: "That was a joke."

Staffer: "…We already put a statement out that said that we were not considering [lockdowns]."

Gavin liked Cuomo, though he couldn't say they'd had much interaction. The tough New Yorker bravado that Cuomo exuded was something most governors could only dream about.

If COVID didn't let up soon, the two men might very well be locked into battle for the 2024 presidential nomination, or even this year's vice presidency.

And for once, it wouldn't be a war of words so much as a war of results: lives saved during a deadly pandemic.

In that spirit of healthy competition, it was time for action, even if Cuomo wasn't ready to pull the trigger. Gavin wouldn't waste time that China, Italy, New Orleans, and New York City wished they'd had before the disease struck. Hearing about events all over the state with early case counts, it was clear that time was short.

Gavin nodded to the director and began his twenty or thirty step walk to the podium while wearing a somber smile, the kind of smile you give to family members at a wake.

"Alright," Gavin muttered under his breath, centering himself, checking to make sure he was live on the monitor, then finally looking dead center into camera.

"Thank you everybody."

The camera lens staring Gavin down began to warp and recede in the way that lenses do when they rapidly zoom directly toward you. The only people that knew anything about that effect were the camera operators themselves, politicians, and news anchors.

As intimidating as the opening zoom might have felt, it had the effect that Gavin thought was a good compliment for his walkup. It helped viewers to focus. It was artistic in a way, and he couldn't take full credit for what the livestream staff had come up with themselves.

"Um, I have long believed that the future is not just something to experience. It's something to manifest."

Reaching out to grab both edges of the podium, and slightly leaning forward, Gavin was suddenly flustered, not entirely sure where to position himself. All he could do was continue speaking, and let the words make the moment.

"We can make decisions to meet moments. And this is a moment we need to make tough decisions. This is a moment where we need some straight talk, and we need to tell people the truth."

Gavin knew that if Cuomo would watch any part of this, he would hear that part loud and clear.

"We need to bend the curve in the state of California. And in order to do that, we need to recognize the reality. The fact is, the experience we're having on the ground throughout the state of California, the experience that's manifesting all across the United States and for that matter, around the rest of the world, requires us to adjust our thinking and to adjust our activities."

The governor's other rival, and a true rival at that, was President Donald Trump, who had formed a love/hate relationship with the governor and California's attorney general in the years since his election, three years prior.

Trump hadn't said a damn thing about widely restricting activities at a federal level, and to Gavin's knowledge, wouldn't take the lead. If Trump wouldn't take action to protect his citizens, Newsom would.

"Now, as I speak, some 21.3 million Californians reside in a community in a city and or county that have similar orders. A state as large as ours…. requires of this moment that we direct a state-wide order for people to stay at home. That directive goes into force and effect this evening."

The directive, executive order N-33-20, wasn't the kind of thing that made for good television. It was a simple order at that, and this speech wasn't about reading orders verbatim.

I as State Public Health Officer and Director of the California Department of Public Health order all individuals living in the State of California to stay home or at their place of residence except as needed to maintain continuity of operations of the federal critical infrastructure sectors.

If Gavin were to read that to the ever-increasing numbers of viewers today, he'd either lose their attention, or worse, increase their panic. The words quarantine and mandate were already sidelined to avoid such possibilities.

"People will ask, well, how will you enforce? As I say, there's a social contract here…. We will have social pressure and that will encourage people to do the right thing, and just to nod and look saying, 'Hey, maybe you should reconsider just being out there on the beach, being twenty-two strong at a park.'"

Gavin liked twenty-two strong. It rolled off the tongue so nicely, and seemed like a small enough number that any large gathering could be maligned, while at the same time directly kneecapping anyone that wanted to get together more than that. That's about as close to specific numbers as he dared get, for fear that his pandemic plan might be restricted by its own guardrails.

The state needed options and might for weeks or months to come.

The enforcement question was a valid one, and one that Gavin hoped to never have to answer. It would be unpopular enough to bring the Golden State to a grinding halt, once the heroism of the moment wore off.

Now, it was time to see whether or not California would fall into line.

"I don't believe that the people of California need to be told through law enforcement that it's appropriate just to home isolate, protect themselves, go about the essential, essential patterns of life."

Cuomo got the message though, enacting New York's stay-at-home order only 24 hours later.

4

TWO MONTHS TO FLATTEN THE CURVE

San Diego, CA – April 2020

Only a few weeks into the pandemic, Amy was already feeling like a broken record.

The disbelieved soothsayer act was one that she had hoped would fall by the wayside as her clients and their vendors grasped the gravity of COVID's dawn. But in many cases, they only dug their heads deeper into the sand.

If Amy had been cursed by Apollo, as the Greek myth of Cassandra goes, she wasn't aware of it, but certainly would not be surprised to find out it had been the case. Her current call with one of her June grooms, Peter, wasn't going any better.

Every couple Amy had planned for had its own idiosyncrasies, and there wasn't any job more difficult than event planning for two people embarking on a life together.

In over a decade, Amy had seen it all.

She had enough horror stories to fill an entire dinner party, not that she would ever divulge client information so flippantly. On top of that, reminiscing was supposed to be about happy moments, not stressful ones.

Nevertheless, Amy certainly wouldn't forget that Caribbean wedding that she agreed to take on, back in the very first weeks of First Comes Love.

That couple had contacted her in the eleventh hour, or rather, what would be considered the eleventh hour in an industry that's so reliant on lead times. Their planner had been forced to drop out because he didn't want to risk making the trip, only to find out he would be trapped outside the United States.

Or that was the couple's story, at least.

It was too early in Amy's business to dart at the first sight of a red flag. Whether in San Diego or somewhere extravagant, income was income. And Amy earned every penny that weekend.

When she'd landed at the airport, the cab had been hours late to pick her up. It's something she'd come to expect, and it's usually the sign of a novice event: people stranded at bus stations, train depots, and airports.

For this reason, Amy joked that wedding guests stranded by their family members made up most of the taxi business, especially with how challenging rideshare pickups had grown at most major airports.

But that's why you hire an event planner—whether that's for a wedding or for anything that takes more than a cake and some streamers: planners think about everything, and they don't just hope for the best. Good event planners are ready for the worst. Yet Amy still wasn't ready for what awaited her after a rough cab ride.

This bride and groom had met on the beach, and not just any beach, but a specific part of a specific beach. Understandably, that was where the bride was determined to celebrate.

Amy had seen her share of beaches, having planned plenty of weddings there, and having enjoyed many more Saturday mornings watching her kids dig sandcastles and search for hermit crabs. Many of San Diego's beaches presented regulatory challenges, and many more of Southern California's beaches were challenged by geography or real estate. Once those hurdles had been hopped, there was always somewhere to set up chairs and a lattice.

But not on this beach.

Amy double- and triple-checked the coordinates as she had paced the area. This couldn't be it, she'd thought. There wasn't even a beach to speak of, nor had there ever been. It was only ocean and shrubs.

Stinky, salty, seaweed-laced shrubs.

The other revolving door of cataclysms that weekend didn't stack up to that moment of defeat, as Amy's shoes began to fill with a mix of sand and sludge.

While most wedding planner horror stories don't end with a bulldozer, this one did. And thanks to that bulldozer's work, not to mention the local authorities' openness to look elsewhere, a beach was created where before there had been none.

The show must go on.

Back in the present, it was Peter (and shortly, Sarah) who would be carving a new scar in Amy's memories.

"Uh, let me put you on with her," Peter mumbled, only after exhausting what Amy assumed was Sarah's written-up list of questions.

A quick scuffle on the other end of the line flooded her ear, as Peter forced the phone into Sarah's hands, no longer wishing to be a middleman.

Sarah's displeasure evaporated as she put on a happy face.

"Hi Amy! This is Sarah!"

"Hi Sarah. I'm not sure if you could hear what Peter and I—"

"Yes! So much. And we appreciate your concern. So, so much."

Amy could finish this part of the conversation easily and would have drawn up her own flowchart if every single one didn't go the exact same way.

"We really don't want to change anything."

"Isn't there another way?"

"Can we just give it another few weeks?"

It didn't get much more varied than that.

She certainly tried, though.

"Sarah, you two need to be prepared, just in case. It's not common for these venues to have extra slots like this so soon, and we're really lucky to be getting all your vendors moved."

Out of all the stages of grief, Amy usually managed to encounter bargaining or depression, but when anger appeared, it was never welcome.

"Amy, no offense, but... but how dare you?"

The nastiness stung, especially after all the hard work Amy had done for Sarah and Peter up until this point. She was working harder these past weeks than she did in the height of wedding season, and this part didn't pay overtime. Force majeure only benefited insurers, it seemed.

"I'm sorry?"

The stereotype of the bridezilla was one Amy desperately hoped to avoid, and usually did. She always tried to give people the benefit of the doubt. You never know when there might be a miscommunication.

But Sarah lashed out again, bellowing, "This is my day. Who are you to change that? Who are you to make me change what I've planned since I was a little girl!?"

Amy didn't know what to say, and was saved by another call, which is a bland excuse, not that any combination of vowels and nouns would make Sarah any less furious.

This call wasn't from a couple or a venue, though, and that made Amy feel like answering would be more fruitful than extinguishing Sarah's rage.

"Sarah, I'm sorry but I'm getting another call. Let me just get right back to you."

Knowing she was throwing Peter to the sharks, Amy put Sarah on hold before she could protest, and swapped the calls.

"Hi, Amy. How are you holding up?"

The voice belonged to Wendy, who owned an events company in National City.

"I'm good. The family is starting to get a little stir crazy," Amy admitted, happy to swap the polite small talk for the verbal lashing that was likely growing on the other line.

"Us too. The kids… well, one day at a time. I wanted to ask about First Comes Love, though. I've been talking with some others around town, and I think everybody thinks you'd have some ideas for how we're going to start making our way out of all this."

Amy laughed a bit. If that was the rumor, she certainly hadn't started it.

"Do they?"

"Well yes, especially with your work with the city and everything."

Amy shrugged, glancing at Ariana as she colored in the newly established (and more accurately, annexed) kids' zone of Amy's L-shaped double desk.

She explained, "I've been trying to get in touch with the city, but I'm only really working with the tourism department, which isn't the same. They just have, like, pointers. And loose ideas."

"Oh, really?"

"Yeah. Sorry."

Wendy went quiet just as Sarah's call appeared on Amy's phone again. She used Wendy's momentary silence to pull the phone from her face and make sure Sarah was still on hold. Too many times, Amy had accidentally made a conference call, and didn't want to make that mistake under such potentially charged circumstances.

"Maybe you'd be willing to join the Facebook group I've put together, and just see if there's something, I mean anything, that can be done."

"Facebook group?"

"Yes! It's called SD Events," Wendy explained, just as the invite appeared in Amy's notifications.

"It's just a place for all of us to get together and share resources. With so many people thinking you might know what was going on, I just thought it was worth sharing it and seeing."

"Thanks, Wendy. Good on you for putting it together."

"I'll make you one of the in-charge people, or admins, or whatever. I mean, if that's OK with you. Don't want to drop a whole new task in your lap."

It didn't seem like there was a choice. The time spent organizing with this group would save time in the long run if it meant getting to reopening soon. The postponement work was starting to add up, and the broken record routine was getting old.

"Fine by me."

Sarah's call dropped a second time just as Amy said goodbye to Wendy, giving Amy a chance to read the handful of posts on the group.

Being a fairly new group, it only took a few minutes for her to read every post and comment that had been made. She saw a good deal of familiar names and faces and recognized even more familiarly the widespread stress over solutions.

The event industry is full of people who like to be prepared, and COVID was the antithesis of that, for every planner, caterer, photographer, and so many others outside what the general public usually considered.

"I posted this in a comment but figured I would post as well," she typed.

"We have been counseling our clients to pick off peak dates…and to check with vendors BEFORE selecting a new date. It's helped immensely with making the process as easy as possible on the couples and the vendors. I am happy to counsel any couples who need help through this completely free of charge. If you have couples struggling who don't have a planner, please feel free to give them my number."

Thirty likes and five or ten comments later, Amy could already tell that, amongst these few group members, people needed answers. Plus, with all the fear of vitriolic conflagrations swirling around, it was nice to see some thank you's and you're awesome's in the reply feed.

Nobody was out to "kill Grandma," yet another accusation that had been floating around.

The group wasn't much, but this was a start, and would hopefully put an end to calls and emails from those who thought Amy would have the answers. It was clear they'd need those answers in short order, and Amy didn't presently have access to those in government who might have them.

In the days and weeks that would follow, though, it was obvious that a refresher on local government would be necessary. Amy wasn't ready to flip through Ariana's social studies textbook to figure out the difference between the mayor, the city, and the county, but she would need to Google as much.

In a perfect world they were all supposed to be on the same page. Yet a perfect city government wouldn't have suffered a pension crisis or lost a major NFL team in the past decades like San Diego had.

Amy's membership in the group quickly engrossed her, allowing her to swap the individualistic phone calls for a hive-mind's collective work, as the afternoon turned to evening, and as that evening turned into the next day.

One name kept coming up over and over again in conversations about getting something done: Brent Dennison.

Brent was an award-winning chef who owned a catering company. Amy had worked with Brent a handful of times, and he'd taken on the unofficial leadership role in the next steps for their disjointed industry.

"Brent is working hard on it."

"Last I heard, he had been chatting with the county people."

"No doubt, Brent has an update soon. He's been 'cooking,' LOL."

Knowing that she might do better helping Brent than trying to go it alone, Amy made it a point to talk with him, and would soon get her chance.

***

"The circumstances… well, you know. But obviously, just happy to know you're still doing all you do. On my end, I'm able to feed the family some great meals for once. They're half wishing I would just run out of business! I'm not. But, yeah. You know, I'm just joking."

Brent was his old self. Even the pandemic couldn't ruin that.

"Well, that's my trouble," Amy explained. "I'm a doer, and don't know what needs doing."

Brent laughed warmly. "I believe it! You moving everything around so far?"

"As best I can. That's why I wanted to reach out. Everyone on the Facebook group was talking about you. Thought I might see how I can help, and I wanted to see what progress you'd made."

He paused.

"Facebook?"

"SD Events. Or something along those lines."

"Ah, sure, right," Brent mumbled, feigning knowledge of what she was talking about.

"It's not important. I feel like I'm in so many Facebook groups these days they all jumble together. I've been helping other planners and venues set up their second and third choice dates, for instance. In case things keep getting pushed back."

"You're doing God's work," Brent admitted.

"But obviously, it's hard to keep doing that when we don't know if this thing is going to be a matter of weeks, or I mean, God forbid, months. That would be horrible, but at least I can throw my hands up and stop treading water here, right?"

Hearing months come out of her mouth was something Amy had been fearing but hadn't said aloud to anyone until just now. It left her with the same internal dread that Brent was doing his best to conceal.

"You and me both. I've got all the food to order too, so I can have this stuff totally spoil if they decide to change something. I've even heard the supply chains are starting to — ugh. It's a mess. I'm nearing my wits' end."

"I'm sure."

There was a pause, the kind of pause that happens when an interviewee and their interviewer haven't kept track of who is whom.

Awkward pauses during phone calls hadn't been harbingers of good things since Amy's call with Paula, and this was shaping up to be another nail in that coffin.

Like turning the key in the ignition to flip over an engine, Amy prodded, "What have you found out?"

Brent sighed, noisily searching beneath binders and stacks of paper on his desk.

"Ah shit, I guess... I can't even find the list. Sorry. I could have pulled it out if I knew that was what you were calling about. Not that I had much written down for it."

"I'm just trying to see if I can help with a few things you've started on. Like, conversations you need help continuing, or people to talk to."

"I haven't talked to anybody, though. Is what I'm trying to say."

Now it was Amy's turn to get quiet.

"Oh."

"Like I said, I'm doing my best, but there's not a lot of—"

"Sure Brent, didn't mean to imply it. You've already helped so much."

"I'm really sorry. I'm going to try to get a start this weekend. I'm just struggling with all of this right now. The PPP loan paperwork is just a beast, and the bank is stuck processing."

"You don't need to explain yourself to anybody, least of all me."

This wasn't cataclysmic, but it wasn't great either. By no fault of Brent, the industry had made him their advocate, and he didn't totally realize it. Even if he did, there wasn't anything he could do about it right now.

"Initiative" was a word that had always stuck with Amy. She always thought that everyone possessed initiative of one kind or another, but in reality, everyone is happier letting someone else take the first step. And when they don't take that step at the right time, the group that volunteered them doesn't usually have a backup plan.

But Amy could exercise some initiative, and a lead time didn't hurt.

"Brent, I'm going to try to tackle this. Just don't let me step on your toes or get in your way."

"That would be great. No worries. I look forward to hearing what you find out. Maybe if I can get my shit together I'll be more help…"

"You know I'll be asking for favors when I need them."

So far, the group project of the San Diego events industry had gone just like any group project might: disjointedly. Now it was time for Amy to pull the all-nighter to get everyone else the grades they needed to pass.

She prepared to hang up the call and get to work.

"Really enjoyed catching up with—"

Brent piped in, having just found his misplaced list.

"Oh, and Amy? I think the real bugger in all this is the county. Not the city or the mayor or the public health people. It's going to be the county you need to talk to. They're the ones in control. I hope that helps."

"It does," Amy nodded, not realizing Brent had put her on a collision course with San Diego's Board of Supervisors.

5

FIRST COMES LOVE'S TRAVEL STOP

North Platte, NE – April 29th, 2020

"Not long ago, a man named Tony Gebeley came to my apartment. Young guy, dark hair, he grew up in New Jersey."

For years, Malcolm Gladwell's Revisionist History podcast had made summer road trips bearable, and almost something to look forward to. I would save the episodes up—as long as a whole year in this case—before finally listening to a season of eight to ten episodes. Like Gladwell's many books, I found his podcast to be excellent, especially in its earliest seasons.

But this wasn't a summer road trip. It was a late spring cross-country move amidst a raging pandemic.

"You're listening to 'Revisionist History,' my podcast about things overlooked and misunderstood. This episode is a special production in honor of America's birthday."

I had hoped to save the lion's share of season 4 for tomorrow, which would be a grueling eight-hundred-mile trek from Colorado Springs, CO to Phoenix, AZ, the third day of four on my and my fiancée's move from Milwaukee to San Diego.

Unfortunately, I had smashed the "in case of emergency" glass a full 22 hours early, already bored by my other options, and my hands starting to get clammy on the plastic steering wheel of our 2005 Hyundai Tucson, which was reliably ferrying me and Kate across western Nebraska.

I could delve into the many quirks of the car, but I think the CarFax said it most succinctly.

"190,000 MILES, REPOSSESSED FROM TWO DIFFERENT OWNERS, AND SPARSE MAINTENANCE RECORD," or something to that effect.

I had a bottom-barrel price target for the car, but we relented a few hundred above that for the sake of collective sanity in the early stages of life together.

"Is the sound turned up all the way?" Kate asked from the passenger seat.

She was the other half of why I enjoyed Revisionist History so much and waited to listen to it like it was an aged wine. Our summers had been full of road trips across the great West, and Gladwell happened to be the territory where our intelligences found common interest.

I reached out to click the side of the phone just to make sure. The little row of Apple-designed white dots confirmed my suspicion.

"Yeah. But I can't really hear either."

"The wind's so loud."

"Sorry. I should have gotten an FM transmitter or something."

The CarFax left out, "VEHICLE LACKS APPLE CARPLAY," though that was to be assumed.

Our final days in Milwaukee had been too hectic for me to consider grabbing a transmitter on the way out. Instead, it was a week of madly selling our furniture in the COVID-free apartment parking lot and begging our landlord not to charge us for carpet cleaning, as it was totally impossible to hire a carpet cleaner at that moment in time.

But all that was literally in the rearview mirror. Soon, COVID would be too, albeit metaphorically.

On the other hand, "two weeks to flatten the curve" was now beginning to seem like it might be four or five weeks, from what I could tell. The city dwellers of New York and San Francisco had a great deal of obedience compared to their suburban and rural counterparts around where we'd lived. While drone videos of creepily empty streets flooded Reddit, I'd looked out our window to see vehicles of all shapes and sizes speeding their way back and forth across W. North Avenue, as if nothing had changed.

On a positive note, the USN hospital ships Mercy and Comfort had provided very little of either to the ports of Los Angeles and New York, where they'd been stationed weeks prior, and were sent back to port in San Diego after only a handful of people stepped onboard.

Case counts were already calming in those cities too, compared to their exponential growth in March.

If things worked out as expected, Kate and I could celebrate our joint Palm Springs bachelor/bachelorette party as close to our original date as possible. Though it was likely that one or two of Kate's bridesmaids would miss the event, likely needed in their hospitals' COVID wards.

Our wedding date, luckily, was about as comfortably far away as one could hope for: August 1st, 2020. While I had heard couples liked to marry on numerically fortuitous dates, I wasn't concerned about fortune. Though it was undeniable that 8/1/2020 was numerically beautiful.

Even as the Naval hospitals departed their posts on East and West coasts, Kate and I did have to consider that our wedding plans could be impacted once "two weeks to flatten the curve" had ended. Kate and I had divided-and-conquered our wedding task list, and March was six months prior to our big day, when most of that Gantt chart triggered.

Like a reckless gambler tossing chips on roulette numbers right and left, not realizing the ball had already landed on double zero, Kate and I had already begun laying down deposits with many of our vendors, while still assembling shortlists for the remaining caterers, musicians, and more.

It was stressful, impending pandemic or not, as any married couple in planning stages can tell you. At the same time, I tried to remind myself we were very privileged to be planning such a big event to, in essence, celebrate both ourselves and our union. Moreover, as practicing Catholics who met at USC's Catholic Center, Kate and I cared deeply about the religious aspect of marriage, and that part was a lot more straightforward than planning the reception.

In the car, another constant of the planning process reared its head: yet another phone call. The rolling series of calls and video chats, whether from family, friends, vendors, or clergy, had only increased. And, such calls had grown more stressed, especially as those individuals began to volunteer their odds we'd be able to marry at all.

I expected a look of dread on Kate's face after she'd said most of the things you hear someone say on one side of a phone conversation:

"Hello!... That's great…. If you think so…. Looking forward to it. Talk to you soon."

Kate wasn't stressed or dreadful when she hung up, though, as she revealed what I already knew.

"That was Amy."

Amy was the only person who could bring a sense of peace to either of us while we planned our nuptials. She was our wedding planner, and a great one.

While most grooms might be concerned with the bachelor party, tuxedo fittings, or their getaway car, my wedding dealbreaker was that I wanted a planner. I'd attended too many weddings where the bride tried to go it alone and ended up saving a small amount of money at the price of her sanity. Not to mention the sanity of her mother, the maid of honor, her husband, and the venue manager. And on and on.

My friend Jack told me, "Rob, the rules of marriage are simple: happy wife, happy life." And I firmly believed the road to a happy wife, especially on Kate's first day with that title, was dependent on having a planner at our sides. With all the nerves that run through any wedding day, a planner would keep the bride from having second thoughts too, right?

"Amy wants to move from her 'day of' to her expanded package, but gave me the option, so we don't have to," Kate informed me. "She's going to have to do a lot of extra work with our vendors, especially if we have to start moving things."

"Can we afford it?" I asked, trying to practice that fiscal responsibility that's comforting to one's spouse-to-be. Though, I already knew my answer to that question, since Amy had already done a great deal of work outside her contract up to this point, and very much deserved a bonus, if not more.

"I certainly think so," Kate said.

"Great. Me too."

Little did we know, not only would Amy be a crucial part of our wedding day, but we wouldn't have been able to marry at all without her.

A mile away, the unmistakable Love's gas station sign towered into the sky, a mainstay for anyone that's driven between longitudes eighty and one hundred-twenty in the United States.

The brilliant folks at the company managed to calculate the precise distance a driver's stomach would begin to growl, their bladder run out of space, or both, and managed to evenly spread Eisenhower's highway network with the precise number of these bright yellow stopovers.

Kate and I agreed it was worth a break, if only to stretch our legs.

The wind wasn't any less intense, stepping out of the Hyundai a minute later. Stretching wasn't as relaxing as a result. But the dollar-per-gallon gas was certainly nice, as I pushed the unleaded button. No doubt gas would rise once "two weeks to flatten" had come to its end.

Returning from her trip to the restroom, just as the fuel finished pumping, Kate motioned to her phone.

"Calling my mom now."

I nodded as I swapped places with her.

Inside the Love's restroom, some early pandemic fears seeped into my head. Trying to lessen any COVID exposure I might encounter, I kept my breathing to as few gulps as possible and made sure to wash my hands for the full twenty seconds recommended by the NIH.

A truck driver in one of the stalls began to have a coughing fit, but it wasn't a COVID cough so much as a smoker's cough, not that I really knew the difference. I held my breath a few extra seconds and washed my hands more quickly, splitting the difference between statistical risks.

While I didn't recall ever wiping our groceries down with sanitizer, I certainly hadn't been innocent of those early pandemic idiosyncrasies.

The wind slapped me across the face as soon as I got back outside. As long as we were in Nebraska, I suspected the gusts would win the fight to keep me from continuing Gladwell's take on the Tea Party.

The pressure in my ears popped as I got back in the driver's seat and the air went still again. I was joining Kate's half of her phone call with her parents, making their daily check-in on our trip's progress.

Kate laughed the sing-song-y laugh that I had fallen in love with years before.

"Oh don't worry, we've got some toilet paper for you. Yeah, Rob found a store-brand bag, right before everybody swarmed. He learned about it from Reddit."

"I don't think it's two-ply," I warned her, under my breath.

There were a lot of unknown toilet paper brands that had surfaced in those days. I didn't think I'd actually seen legit Cottonelle in a month.

Kate waved it off. Her mom had been stockpiling the stuff for years. We'd be well prepared for our next three weeks staying with her parents in our first true COVID pod.

For all the toilet paper and hand sanitizer shortages I expected to encounter in San Diego, I was grossly unprepared for what California had in store: required movement on public beaches, masking outdoors in all cases, and partial or complete closures of public parks.

While the prospects of a bachelor party dwindled as May commenced (and commencement ceremonies did not), Kate and I would begin to receive our first cancellations, even if they were soft ones.

We didn't think so highly of ourselves that we expected everyone to attend, even under non-COVID circumstances. Most of the cancellations that would come were totally understandable. The few that were from friends or family who'd traveled on exotic trips throughout the pandemic would hurt, though, purely due to the half-truths they volunteered.

But that was in the weeks to come. In the moment, Kate wrapped up her second call, checking the map on my phone.

"We'll let you know when we get to Denver, or wait, it's Colorado Springs. Is that the same? Or they're... like forty-five minutes apart. Right. Love you too!"

Kate hung up and laid back for a nap before we reached Ogallala, where she was going to start her next leg of driving. Growing up with Texas and Louisiana road trips, the middle-of-nowhere towns didn't sound much weirder to me than your average Ruston, Bogalusa, or Biloxi, but Ogallala was certainly up there.

"Anything I can play for you?" Kate asked.

I shrugged, "Don't want to finish Boston Tea Party without you. Music is fine, I guess. My 2017 playlist."

"OK."

I confessed, "The guy in my bathroom was coughing a lot. I held my breath as much as I could."

"Less viral load! Good for you," she smirked, as Modest Mouse's Float On started.

Unlike a new episode of a podcast, I had this tune memorized. The wind could do its worst.

6
THE CAPE'D CRUSADER

San Diego, CA – May 2020

There was a time before Amy knew the names Jim Desmond, Nathan Fletcher, Greg Cox, Dianne Jacob, and Kristin Gaspar. Those five members of San Diego's 2020 Board of County Supervisors stood at the inevitable conclusion of Amy's springtime efforts to forge a path forward.

Those efforts had started small. She'd tried to work smart and hard, rather than just the latter of the two.

First, Amy had thought it worth double-checking, wanting to make sure someone else hadn't taken up this banner on a national level. An email from her contact at the Association of Bridal Consultants and a call with Serena at San Diego NACE, the National Association for Catering and Events, confirmed that.

In essence, what the organizations had told Amy wasn't bad news, but it couldn't really be considered good news either. It was another step forward, if nothing else. And it would mean more work for Amy in the near term, assuming she wanted to bring her business back to life again, the business she'd built with her blood and sweat over the past decade. Was she just supposed to pivot from a decade at First Comes Love to something totally new, like others had already been forced to do?

The call with Serena didn't last nearly as long as Amy had expected. Once again, Amy's laundry list of talking points was futile.

Serena volunteered, "Our hands are tied, and it's been really frustrating. I'm sure you can imagine."

Amy nodded, beginning to type notes as she put her phone on speaker. Though, there wasn't much to type. Instead, Serena fumbled through what she knew about non-profit designations. Quick searches on Charity Navigator and ProPublica weren't going to yield quick answers.

"What would you need to be able to take the NACE cause to the city or state level?"

"Nothing. We can't. The association isn't the right kind of 501 to take action. If you have any idea what the difference is. Because I just learned myself."

Unfortunately for Amy, this wasn't going to show up in any of her children's social studies homework, which happened to be sprawled across the end of her L-shaped home office desk.

Guidestar had some help a few milliseconds later with the following: "Business leagues, chambers of commerce, real estate boards, etc., created for the improvement of business conditions."

Adding, "Donations to this organization are not tax deductible."

Being familiar with 501(c)(3) entities, especially in the last days of each calendar year when her inbox was flooded with their entreaties for end-of-year donations, Amy had always assumed there were other flavors of 501(c). Although she had hoped they would be equally tax deductible.

"I see," Amy answered. "I'm guessing there's an entity that can do what we need, then?"

"That's right! I don't know the right number, but it's there," Serena said. "I'm happy to ask our guy here, if you need it."

It was the opposite of a dead end. It meant having to do an about-face.

"That's alright, Serena. I'm on it."

Even with this mythical 501, it wasn't clear what Amy would be able to do with the organization if she took the time to start it. She needed to make good contact with someone more powerful than their homeowner's association president, yet more local than the governor.

And that's where Jim, Nathan, Greg, Dianne, and Kristin would come in.

***

It had taken hours of research and internet sleuthing with every spare moment Amy could spare between client calls, vendor "re-reschedulings," and taking the ever more restless E.J. and Ariana for walks around their neighborhood.

The walks around the neighborhood featured those awkward encounters with neighbors relying on the same source of exercise. Amy and the kids would approach others and do a little dance at a distance, deciding which family would be the one to throw themselves into oncoming traffic to avoid the possibility of spreading asymptomatic coronavirus.

Summer vacation inevitably threatened to unleash kids on their parents not just for nights and weekends, but also around the clock. Not that video conference school had occupied them nearly as much as in-person learning once had. It felt like summer vacation should be coming to an end, not starting anew.

Luckily, Amy had been able to piece together a layman's understanding of the governmental powers that stood between her and a return to her work/life balance, in spite of the looming summer break.

The basics were all easy. San Diego was founded just after the Mexican-American War in 1850. Familiar names like Juan Carbillo and Junipero Serra and tribal names like the Kumeyaay and Utay/Otay adorned many of San Diego's commemorative parks, rivers, and highways.

As the 19th century turned to the 20th, the power dynamics of California got more complicated. First, the state established not one, but two, types of counties. The larger counties like San Diego and Los Angeles are considered charter counties and have more power than what are called "general law" counties.

All counties have a good deal of power in California, especially in areas of the law not specified by the state. Pandemic policy was one such area.

Second, cities and counties have crossover, but not like Amy had expected when she first sought out San Diego city staff. Cities were designed to operate, whereas counties were the ones designated to legislate. Kevin Faulconer might have been the well-known mayor of San Diego, but when Amy reached out to his staff, their tune was similar to the tourism board's: they had to wait on guidance.

The leaders of San Diego County operated over a far wider swath of the population than just the alphabetized downtown streets from "A" to "Epsilon." The city was a little over a million in population, but the county was easily three. And the county didn't have one person at its head. It had five.

At last, all those campaign billboards lining Torrey Pines Road had some meaning. "County Supervisor" had seemed so insignificant, in between red and blue signs for "treasurer" and "insurance commissioner." But no longer. For a short moment in time, the county supervisors had more control than the governor or president.

Amy wished that the county and the city had been given different names, akin to Oakland and Alameda County. But for most of California's chartered counties, the county name was made to match the city it encompassed, citizen access be damned.

There was one paragraph that stood out most during Amy's research, this one on the CSAC website, the association representing California's counties:

"Unlike the separation of powers that characterizes the federal and state governments, the Board of Supervisors is both the legislative and the executive authority of the county. It also has quasi-judicial authorities."

And that sounded A-OK with her. The federal government's checks and balances had made COVID policy such a nightmare by now that it had already been mostly delegated to the states. Amy didn't want to go down this path if it meant getting derailed by some judge along the chain of command.

It was going to be all or nothing.

While the 501(c) paperwork was in process, and she was rallying her troops, Amy could at least start her work as an involved citizen. She commented on a video from Nathan Fletcher, District 4's supervisor, on May 20th:

"Question: Any update on weddings and when they will be able to resume and at what guest count to start?"

Fletcher responded, "Not yet. We did funerals as a first step. Hang in there."

"Hang in there" was one of those pandemic platitudes that had already begun to grow stale. Soon, "we're all in this together" would vie for the top spot, used well into the years that followed.

The SD Events Facebook group had quickly grown into a crucial pillar in the fight to bring events back to San Diego, and as May progressed, Amy found more allies in the ranks of the caterers, planners, photographers, and deejays put out of work, many of whom knew pandemic unemployment was already on the congressional chopping block, and their survival with it.

It was two weeks earlier that Amy had seen the tides beginning to shift. "Two weeks to flatten the curve" had ended around week five or six in flyover states and had begun its wane in California in weeks eight to ten, especially as summer weather returned.

One of Amy's early posts that didn't make her personal Facebook feed, yet she felt encouraged to post within the events group, was a mashup of screenshots she'd taken of polls from the Instagram account Betches Brides, which showed an informal count of how couples felt about weddings, depending on the 2020 month during which they'd marry.

Just in the first couple weeks of May, the rotating poll showed a 10-15% shift toward brides choosing not to postpone weddings between August and December. It was one of the first signs of the direction that younger people were taking in this chapter of the pandemic. Their bullishness would only increase as outdoor temperatures climbed and case counts declined.

The Facebook group also became a place to vent frustrations or to ask for help. On May 13th, Amy had queried without shame, "Are any of you looking into alternate sources of income or employment? All of my 2020 is pushing and I feel like there's just no way to sustain in this current environment."

And the replies spoke volumes:

"If you can sustain by plugging away at your 'real' job, working on marketing and sales to build your business, this will be much more beneficial in the long run than earning minimum wage at a job that is nothing related to your primary occupation. I've committed to keep pushing through."

And,

"I definitely don't have it in me to do virtual events so I'm looking into going back to having a regular corporate job. I won't turn down a wedding, but I don't see an end to this before my money runs out."

As well as "My local grocery store was hiring, so I'm trying that out."

But the day after Fletcher's request that Amy "hang in there," Amy had had enough. Summer break was only three weeks away, and cases were on the decline. Another month with no industry recognition and summer could be lost in its entirety.

"Hi all: Not to be one to 'stir the pot,' actually, yes, I am trying to stir the pot... I kindly ask that you make your voice heard as a member of the San Diego wedding community that we start getting some communication and guidelines from the county on weddings and events, when they will be allowed and capacities once the restrictions are loosened."

The letter she'd included with the post would be one of the first sent to county leadership and anyone else who would listen, including the email address <COVID19BusinessQuestions@sdcounty.ca.gov>, which was as long as it was unhelpful.

"If we do not receive guidance in the next week, it is likely that thousands of weddings will postpone or cancel for the fall/winter, which will devastate venues, restaurants, hotels and the entire wedding community who rely on events. So if weddings may be allowed, we need to know. On the flip side, if weddings will not be allowed, that information would be helpful so that we can properly advise our clients of that information and make plans to move forward."

It wasn't a plea to open the floodgates, nor was it a demand to lock down the county for the foreseeable future. It was a request for leadership and consistency. It was a request for a government that would serve its citizens with the guidance they'd so delegated.

On May 29th, Amy posted to the Facebook group again.

"Ok, finally got to the bottom of the local offices that are working on implementing state guidelines at the county level. I'm about to write a strongly worded email directly demanding information on event guidelines and to be kept in the loop as these guidelines are formed. I want to CC as many of my industry friends on this as possible. Please comment or DM me your email if you are interested in me CC'ing you on the request. Once I do send, please reply to help make sure our message is heard!"

Comments on Fletcher's Facebook were just the beginning, and were followed by correspondence with county officials, email campaigns to county supervisors, and even strategy with the mayor and his wife.

Finally, Amy's email received a new approval message from the secretary of state: "Your registration of The California Association for Private Events has been approved."

Thanks to the work done by Amy and her fellow six board members, CAPE was born.

One final clause in CSAC's informational site suggested the inevitable next step.

"An official act of the Board of Supervisors can only be performed in a regularly or specially convened meeting. The individual members have no power to act for the county merely because they are members of the Board of Supervisors."

With her newly established board backing her, it was time for Amy to take on the County Board at last.

7

THE BATTLE FOR SAN DIEGO

San Diego, CA – 8:30 a.m., June 23rd, 2020

Second only to 1803's Battle of San Diego Bay, 1846's Battle of San Pasqual, and 1981's AFC Championship Game, the June 23rd San Diego Board of Supervisors meeting could go down in history as one of the city's most hotly contested struggles. Though Amy hoped it wouldn't get too heated.

The county meeting—part in-person and part tele-conferenced—would run a total of six hours, twenty-two minutes, and thirty-five seconds, covering a total of 28 total items, ranging from "fostering academic success in education" (item twelve) to "establishing an office of equity and racial justice" (item twenty-seven).

It was item four, classified under "health and human services," which the California Association for Private Events had fought so hard to have included. It was titled, "RECEIVE UPDATE ON THE COVID-19 RESPONSE, RATIFY ACTIONS AND AUTHORIZE ANY OTHER ACTION NECESSARY TO ADDRESS THE COVID-19 PANDEMIC, AND ESTABLISH APPROPRIATIONS TO SUPPORT PROPOSED ACTIONS."

An asterisk implied that a presentation would accompany this particular talking point. A long list of registered commenters on the county's website implied that the public's input on the topic would require quite a bit of time too.

That morning had been phone calls upon phone calls, upon more video chats and calls. Amy missed the days of face-to-face meetings, because even the very best of video chats felt lacking in getting her point across.

Jim Desmond had been a great help, solely in their corner. Additional morning meetings with Kristin Gaspar, Greg Cox, Dianne Jacob, and Nathan Fletcher yielded a mixed bag by comparison.

Loose ends never left good results in event planning, politics, or on the field of battle. If this vote failed, Amy would have to go back to square one, and in all honesty, she didn't know what that looked like. As July loomed, she'd already lost a summer of weddings, and didn't want that to continue rolling onward, especially with June 12th's slew of reopenings, which spanned what felt like every industry except theirs.

No doubt, June 12th had made her list of talking points that morning. San Diego had given a yellow—if not totally green—light to most industries. Weddings and churches lagged substantially as gyms, restaurants, and even bars flung their doors back open again, spilling into the city's sunny streets and sidewalks.

Waking up in the early hours of Tuesday the 23rd was the conclusion of a long weekend of preparation. Working Fridays, Saturdays, and Sundays wasn't anything out of the ordinary for an event planner, a small business owner, or even an entrepreneur turned political activist. In the same way that she did Tuesday, Amy had brewed a pot of coffee the prior Friday morning and opened the now all-too-familiar Facebook group.

Once an informal information-sharing space, SD Events was now CAPE's army of nearly a thousand San Diego event professionals and their extended client lists and networks.

Staring at the blinking cursor, she'd typed, "The San Diego County Board of Supervisors will be voting on recommending reopening additional businesses at its meeting Tuesday, June 23rd, at 9:00 a.m."

But that had felt bland. In an age of algorithms and digital overload, that wasn't going to rally enough troops, if they even saw it at all.

Amy added, "ACTION NEEDED ON TUESDAY - PRE-REGISTER NOW." That already felt better. And folks saw it:

"What will be the time limit for each comment?"

"Hoping this passes and allows us to get back to normalcy!"

It was over the weekend that her fear of failure began to mount, though. Wilma Wooten, San Diego's Public Health Officer since 2007, was another formerly little-known government member that now held great power compared to others in her agency's history.

San Diego's Board of Health was established in 1869 to handle outbreaks of smallpox. In 1918, the department was elevated into the spotlight again to handle the Spanish Flu, when it urged the public to avoid crowds and distributed flu masks to high schoolers.

The department had been absorbed into the Health and Human Services Agency just before the turn of the century. Now, it would be the source of expertise for the coming meeting. Dr. Wooten's advice, akin to that of the nationally recognized Dr. Anthony Fauci, could sway supervisor votes. And Dr. Wooten's words that weekend hadn't left Amy with a great deal of confidence.

The *L.A. Times and San Diego Union-Tribune* reported on June 22nd, "Wooten said such private gatherings in homes, where people are less inclined to wear masks, would likely be banned under the public health order until herd immunity could be achieved, and that was unlikely to happen this year."

Amy had reached out to update everyone. She had anticipated their concerns.

"There has been some concern voiced about the comments Dr. Wooten made about gatherings, where she said that people should not host others at their homes. We are working with the county reopening team to see if they can clarify that at the next daily briefing to 'unregulated gatherings.'"

It sounded so simple, but as would soon be the case, nothing about lobbying this government was straightforward. The requests, meetings, and even guarantees never held the weight that they did in business dealings.

In her first month of politicking, Amy had found that many politicians were even more fickle than she might have previously guessed. Whether it was the faux listening routine or the outright lie, Amy had found the past month of conversations to be even more infuriating than she'd braced herself for.

The lies were just that: half-truths masked by pearly white rows of perfectly aligned teeth. Any small business owner worth their salt knew a lie from a mile away. Clients and vendors both had made Amy a veteran at deciphering fact from fiction.

But meetings with county supervisors, mayoral staff members, and public health officials weren't as easy as your average groom claiming he'd just misplaced his boutonnière.

It was the career fast talkers that proved to be the most challenging, especially when they seemed to listen so well. When someone "hears you" or "understands," they very well might, and they very well might want to get you out of their office. Over a video conference, that's as simple as clicking a button and sending the CAPE board into a state of digital purgatory.

Today had been a good deal of listening, but Amy was pleased with the repeated assurances the board had been able to secure.

Her final estimation matched the same she'd started with on Tuesday. Jim Desmond would be a yes. Cox and Gaspar would likely both be yeses. Jacob was on the fence, and Fletcher wasn't going to play ball.

Dianne Jacob's meeting that morning gave Amy the most pause, alongside Dr. Wooten's comments from that weekend. If Jacob were to vote nay, it could sway the other yeses too. The worst possible outcome might be an extensive review of the topics at hand, only to have some data set convince the entire board that the guidance was a bridge too far.

Amy tried not to think of all those outcomes as she put forth her own comment in the online form, registered to speak, and prepared for the county live cast to begin.

The Facebook group featured one final post.

"If you are registered, time to call in now!"

***

Chandler, AZ – 8:50 a.m.

Mary Star of the Sea Catholic Church of La Jolla isn't the most well-known church named "Mary Star of the Sea" in California, and barely makes the top five, if one were to somehow rank them. The number one spot undoubtedly belongs to the church of the same name in San Pedro, which dates back to the 1880's.

La Jolla's Mary honorific was built in 1937 in the mission revival style that had shaped many of San Diego's buildings of the early 20th century and survived to this day alongside the gorgeous Balboa Park district, which was partially designed by Mary Star of the Sea's architect, Carleton Monroe Winslow.

The beauty of this style meant that, unlike many of the massive cathedrals and basilicae that serve millions of Catholic worshippers every Sunday, Mary Star of the Sea was small, peaceful, and intimate. At its maximum capacity, the church might be able to fit three hundred worshippers beneath its low roof, stained glass windows, and exposed wooden beams.

The wooden pews creaked in a way that stirred memories of generations of community-centric Catholics gathering in towns and neighborhoods of all sizes, especially across the entire Western Hemisphere. They were distant from the cathedrals of Europe, yet still recited the same hymns and celebrated identical rites to the rest of the globe.

Mary Star of the Sea had become a favorite for me and Kate as we dated in the years leading up to our engagement. Kate had attended their elementary school almost two decades earlier. They'd been our first phone call after getting engaged in 2019, and we'd planned every part of our wedding around the church.

The other importance of Mary Star of the Sea was that to be truly married in the eyes of the Catholic Church, you had to be married at the altar. The Catholic Church isn't building altars on beaches, in ski resorts, or most other destination wedding locales, which means Catholic weddings solely happen indoors.

Moreover, this process meant more documents, organization, and planning than some other faiths or denominations, because marrying at a Catholic church requires more than just cutting a check. On the contrary, especially if you're a member of a given parish, the decreased costs to marry can be outweighed by the hurdles of liturgical paperwork. We were also blessed to have Sunday School teachers and home parish offices who had diligently preserved our church documents, helping us avoid a mad dash through the RCIA process.

Thanks to our consistent churchgoing as children and young adults, combined with our lack of prior marriages (which can present challenges with annulments), getting married at a Catholic church wouldn't be the challenge that it could have very well turned into.

It was the fond memories of Mary Star of the Sea that flooded my mind the afternoon of a different phone call, one which hadn't been on our wedding planning Gantt chart. Amy had texted me about the county meeting a few days prior when I'd reached out to ask if I could help with any of her work, which I'd seen on Facebook and over email.

While it seemed like a lot of political hubbub, a request to another political body to fulfill a request to outline information, this was still the role of government: to determine and execute the will of those that elected them.

In theory, at least.

"We'd love to have you speak, if you're willing," Amy had told me. "We have a lot of chamber of commerce people, but there's a human element to your story. I think I only have a few other actual couples who will call in."

"Any way I can help," I'd pledged.

Amy's pursuit of small business fairness was a cause I was passionate about myself after years of my own entrepreneurial struggles, albeit at a smaller scale.

First, that meant following a link to register to speak during the meeting, which also asked for an online comment.

For a government website, the San Diego County Supervisors had done an above average job in the UI/UX arena. Thanks to their selection of boldface and hyperlinked text, the following made sense:

"If you would like to provide oral comments BY PHONE to the Board of Supervisors during the upcoming Board meeting, please complete the form below prior to the time that public comment begins on the item. Alternatively, you can submit an eComment, which is the most direct way to voice your opinion for a Board of Supervisors agenda item."

Kate and I both opted for the online comment, while I took it upon myself to pursue the call-in option as well. I didn't pretend to know much more about these sorts of meetings, other than what I'd learned from Parks and Recreation episodes or 2017's viral video of Tom Allen's "surfer bro" petitioning the Beverly Hills City Council against a house party ban.

With help from a PDF that CAPE had authored, I typed, "On behalf of small business owners, newlyweds, and congregations across the city, I ask the council to support this cause, so that these groups have a fighting chance against the obvious influence of lobbyists and tax revenue generators."

From her desk in our living room, Kate asked, "How long will it all take?"

I didn't want to sound clueless, considering I could be at this for the next couple hours. I wanted to reply with something knowledgeable and impress her.

"I'm not sure," was all that came out.

She smiled and nodded.

"I'll be at work over here, if you need me!"

The county meeting livestream was as impressive as their website design and launched just after the top of the hour. Alongside the simulcast of the meeting was a presentation showing the document that held meeting notes.

The County News Center simulcast the council chambers with a mirrored view of agenda items and even a picture-in-picture of video call speakers, which included callers with comments and the five supervisors themselves. The physical room featured no fewer than ten county leaders, including Dr. Wooten, each of whom were separated by an empty seat in between each of them.

These in-person attendees each wore masks of varying comfort levels, per the state's current order on indoor measures. Quizzically, this included at least one type of mask, a gaiter, that would later be found to spread COVID at a higher rate than simply leaving one's face uncovered. (That information was thanks to research done by Duke University and would be released later that summer.)

Chairman Greg Cox opened the meeting, "Good morning. I call this meeting of the San Diego County Board of Supervisors to order for Tuesday, June 23rd, 2020," and clacked a gavel on his desk. His computer microphone did not handle the impact with high fidelity, and the room was momentarily filled with an unpleasant, peaking clack.

Cox wore a suit and tie and had white hair. He sat behind a desk in a simple blue room, three flags behind him. He was a Republican and the former mayor of Chula Vista, who had represented San Diego County's first district the longest of any of the board members, since around the time I had been born in the 1990's.

The county clerk, one of the in-person attendees, removed his mask, already dangling from one ear as he waited for the introduction to end, and called the roll, adding, "I'll remind members of the public that have requested to speak to wait to dial into the meeting until the item is called."

Waiting for the right moment to dial in was a challenge, having never done it before. But the meeting interface made it somewhat easier. On a separate screen was located the seal of the county, over it in white text read, "AGENDA ITEM / A. Roll Call." All I had to do was wait for item four, as Amy had instructed.

The roll call gave a first look at the other supervisors. Dianne Jacob, the second-longest serving of the board's members, responded with "Aye," before grinning and fixing her own error. "I mean, here."

In addition to her own chuckle, county staff visible in the room also smiled and laughed, though it was unclear who was doing which, due to the masks covering everything but their raised cheekbones and squinting eyes.

Jacob wore a blue blouse and a necklace beneath a black blazer. Known as "East County's Iron Lady," Jacob had never lost a campaign for her seat, which encompassed almost a third of the county's total land area, between the International Border, Imperial County, and District 5, to the North.

Supervisor Kristin Gaspar of District 3, which contained La Jolla and most of the other coastal areas, did not appear on camera during the meeting, nor was she present when her roll was called.

Nathan Fletcher followed next. He was the board's lone Democrat at the time, having been a Republican until 2013, when he joined the Democratic party after a short stint as an Independent.

His emailed announcement to his supporters in May of that year had read, "Our life experiences contribute greatly to how we view the world. In the last decade I went to war, became a father, governed in a period of great economic crisis and am now preparing to put two children in public school. I've sat with janitors who can't afford healthcare, small business owners struggling to make ends meet, attended services for cops killed in the line of duty, met dreamers who are in the only country they have ever known and sat in classrooms with teachers doing the best they could in a tough environment."

Today, Fletcher opened curtly: "Fletcher, here."

He would first appear on camera during segment "D," titled "Proclamations and Awards." His office, like Cox's, sported the flags of the county, state, and country to one side, as well as personal and professional photos on the other, which formed a collage around a larger poster featuring the 36th President that read, "VIVA LBJ."

He wore a white button-down shirt with a blue tie and black rimmed glasses. His hair was slicked back in a way reminiscent of the state's governor, but with fewer gray hairs. Fletcher represented the densely populated neighborhoods just north of Cox's downtown area.

Coincidentally enough, Kate had interned for Fletcher when he was a state assembly candidate. When I told her he would be one of the pivotal voters in today's meeting, she'd found it humorous.

If there's anything to be learned from this experience, it was that San Diego was its own surprisingly small world.

Jim Desmond was the fifth and final member to proclaim, "Here!"

In a sign of the times, Desmond's audio buffered and emerged horribly warped, sounding more like "rrr-he-rrr."

Quorum had been reached, regardless, and the meeting was now underway.

After the invocation provided by a very San Diegan-looking pastor donning a Hawaiian shirt, and a proclamation that June 23rd would be the county's Racial Justice Coalition of San Diego Day, item one was on deck. But it didn't take long for not only item one, but also items two and three to be tossed aside to get to the meat of the morning's activities, item four.

Cox impatiently suggested, in his gravelly voice, which he explained was the result of recent vocal cord surgery, "If neither one of those speakers are ready to go, then I guess we will move on to item four, at least in here the staff presentation. And if those two speakers call in, we can pick them up after the staff presentation on item four."

Moments later, the County News Center chyron transformed to reveal, "ITEM 4: UPDATE ON THE COVID-19 RESPONSE."

I hoped the rest of the meeting would proceed as easily. The clerk gave the green light, doing the fast talk that was reminiscent of so many radio commercial disclaimers.

"Any members of the commission speaking on this item, please dial into the conference line now using the instructions provided to you and you will be muted until it is your turn to speak."

If the clerk had added, "No purchase necessary to win, must be eighteen years or older, does not apply to residents of Maine, Nevada, and the Solomon Islands," I might not have noticed.

I dialed the "858" area code into my iPhone and entered the call room, where the meeting proceeded on speakerphone.

The Assistant Chief Administrator opened, speaking about increasing numbers of testing sites, followed by Dr. Wooten, who spoke about safety for long-term care facilities, prisons, and the homeless. Wooten then presented on increased testing for vulnerable communities and finished with updated data on COVID spread, which had begun to climb again in tandem with the reopenings and gatherings from earlier in the month.

Luckily, the county was not exceeding state metrics for intervention. If the county exceeded or fell below the state's guidelines for any of the following, the state would take action: average tests per day, case rate, testing positivity, percent change in hospitalizations, and percentage available of ICU beds or ventilators.

But there was one metric that was deficient, a particularly relevant one: community outbreaks.

"As of yesterday, we had ten community outbreaks. Most are businesses and there are three that are private residences," Wooten explained.

She would add that an eleventh had just been registered as part of a "backyard barbeque."

"The team also continues to meet with and advise associations that represent sectors and businesses that are currently not allowed to reopen, in order to advocate to the state on their behalf. However…due to the increased number of community outbreaks after last Friday, our plan is to curtail any additional reopenings until the number of outbreaks decrease."

Thanks to seven businesses and four-and-a-half house parties, it sounded like CAPE was already caught in the muck. Not to mention, it all seemed like a catch-22. Were the businesses that had caused seven outbreaks in the week still open or might they belong to industries encouraging unregulated indoor proximity? Were the residential outbreaks one of the many events that dodged public spaces, which could have been regulated?

The "Reopening in San Diego County" slide listed everything from massage therapy to community pools, not to mention gyms, bars, and wineries. Yet the final bullet point, for places of worship, only read "expanded guidelines," including outdoor services. When it came to reopening San Diego, churches and weddings had been almost exclusively short-changed.

With the formal presentation over, Supervisor Cox readied the county leadership for what would come next.

"My understanding, at least at the start of the meeting, was we had 83 speakers. It would be my intent to ask the speakers to confine themselves to two minutes. In fact, if they can do it in less than two minutes, that's even better."

The clerk revealed that in fact, there were only forty-nine callers still remaining, in addition to 192 e-comments that had been submitted prior to the meeting.

I did the math. If I were the 49th caller (or worse, the 83rd), and each caller got two minutes, this could take another hour-and-a-half. Not to mention sticking around to find out the result of the vote.

I hoped that I wouldn't be 49th. Soon, I realized that I wouldn't be very far off.

The speaker announced, "Our first caller is 0550."

"Good morning," a man on the other end of the line said, a green telephone icon filling the screen as sounds of rustling filled the audio feed.

This caller was on behalf of a San Diego hotel management company and provided a remarkably concise argument for the industry's extreme need for help.

"Two hundred days a year…we depend on business, travel, and meetings to fill our rooms…. Catering events and group business is generally booked three to eighteen months ahead of time. Summer is prime time for catered events, especially outdoor events such as weddings and receptions. The time to book this business is rapidly coming to a close. Similarly, bookings for group business for this summer and fall must start now. Leisure business will not sustain us after mid-August…. I urge you to continue reopening hotel services. We are prepared to do so safely."

The next caller, an assembly candidate who worried about her children losing time in the classroom, had a phone number ending in 0585. With a phone number in the 9000's, I accepted I wasn't going to speak anytime soon.

On the plus side, Amy and CAPE's army had assembled in force.

As the comments continued, it struck me just how many businesses and groups were struggling with the restrictions, and so many outside of weddings and events.

The third caller hit on runaway events, and the risks to outbreak statistics that they caused: "What we're seeing at venues is that people are canceling their current events because of the uncertainty and unknowing of what's happening. And they're going into backyard private weddings or private neighborhoods…. We're asking that we understand there's a number in increase currently, but in a couple of months from now, to allow these events to take place so that we don't lose the back half of the year from those that had moved from spring and early summer."

A fourth caller asked for guidelines that matched "bars, restaurants, casinos, [and] entertainment places."

Speakers seventh, eighth, and ninth asked for a resumption of outdoor fairs so that cottage industries could survive, and with guidelines that matched those for street marches or beach gatherings.

Many of the comments like these were concise, crucial, and reflected the immense challenges faced by San Diego's struggling wedding industry and small businesses at large.

Almost two hours into the meeting, the speaker called a number in the 1500's.

"Good morning, distinguished supervisors and county leaders. Thank you for your dedicated service and time this morning. My name is Amy Ulkutekin and I am a local event planner and owner of First Comes Love and Catalyst Creative. I'm also spearheading the private event sector's reopening efforts for San Diego. As my colleagues have mentioned, we strongly urge you to support the reopening of privately held social events."

Amy's enunciation was as impeccable as her pacing, which sounded like a gatling gun firing at full speed. Every syllable made a forceable impact in a way that the other callers hadn't managed to capture. Her logic was concise and certainly sounded infallible to those of us rooting for her.

"I've been working with all of you directly, or your staff, and hope you have had the opportunity to review the guidelines for events that we've put together to ensure our safe reopening…. Our industry has a much longer lead time than other industries. We need action now."

Every now and then, Amy would hit on a certain word, just so her syntax didn't move at the exact same cadence. It made it so the listeners would have a moment to digest her words in the time it took her to reload and resume the salvo.

"While we recently had the trigger point for community outbreaks, we need to ask Governor Newsom for the ability to reopen events now, so that when the county stabilizes, we can move forward quickly to reopen private events. Additionally, events are happening. They just are in people's backyards. So as an industry we're terrified of these unsanctioned events that are throwing caution to the wind, and not complying with guidelines. Our plans will help to mitigate this and keep San Diegans safe by allowing event professionals to manage these guidelines."

And with that, her speech was finished, and no less than thirty seconds before her time might have expired. While I was still seven or eight thousand numbers away, her words were like lightning to the cause. It wouldn't be hard to wait as long as I still might have to.

Amy's words sounded like they'd come from a place of familiarity with the supervisors. Ever since her comment on Fletcher's video the month prior, she'd had an ongoing dialogue with these members. No doubt, those meetings had been far more involved.

For all the mentions they'd gotten, the runaway events were no joke, and in my own small way, I had been a culprit of the very same for my bachelor weekend. We had obediently downsized from a group of ten in Palm Springs to me and my three brothers at an Airbnb in Scottsdale.

It was one of the earlier days in June when we'd officially pulled the plug on Palm Springs, especially after reading the Cathedral City, CA council meeting notes.

"The Temporary Suspension of all Short-Term Lodging Facility Rentals will continue through June 24, 2020," the city council agenda minutes read.

This date conveniently landed five days after the first federally recognized Juneteenth would be celebrated, and only 48 hours after the Juneteenth holiday weekend would end. Even more coincidentally, Emergency Order 2D was in fact rescinded during that June 24th city council meeting.

As far as I'm aware, the tourism industry of the greater Palm Desert was able to recover without the revenue from our planned trip. And our sibling group didn't ferry any COVID across state lines.

Already demonstrated by the backyard barbecues, there were almost certainly events outside of San Diego at this time that obstructed the county's meaningful pandemic gains, especially due to larger runaway event attendees returning to town and spreading disease on a scale of tens or hundreds.

As phone number one thousand's turned to two's and three's, I texted Amy, "Great speech earlier! My number starts with a nine, so let me know if there are any concluding points you'd like me to add."

She replied, "Can you reiterate that we need action now for future planning and that you as a groom are willing to modify your wedding to be able to move forward?"

"Absolutely."

She added that I shouldn't be afraid to use some emotion.

Even in her own speech, and especially in the rest, emotions had ceded to economic arguments. My interests were the opposite. Canceling our wedding for COVID would have been the best economic decision we'd made in years, if we'd chosen to do so.

In reality, I didn't know how any of my emotions would emerge, beyond the fact that I had plenty on the subject. Whatever I did or said when 9001 arrived, I wouldn't shed crocodile tears.

After another hour of colorful comments, including petitions for reopening playgrounds, resumptions of rowing competitions, and no less than one unfortunate doxxing attempt of Dr. Wooten, the clock wound down on the 8000's.

As each digit advanced, a few more callers had been forced to drop off for sake of time. For the twelve callers in the 1000's, there were only five in the 8000's. And that block also featured the first engaged couple, of which I would represent the second and final.

That bride-to-be noted, "We heard in the presentation today that one of the outbreaks was linked to an outdoor barbecue. I know many other brides who plan on moving forward with their receptions with private residences if they cannot move forward with their venue."

That was when Kate stuck her head in the door.

"Everything OK?"

"Yeah, I'm almost up."

"Wow, it's been hours."

"Three, but who's counting?" I shrugged.

Kate smiled and returned to her living room office, promising to bring me lunch if the meeting stretched to hours four or five.

Public speaking was never a fear of mine, but that didn't mean some nerves didn't help boost my energy levels. My last speech had taken place four months ago in front of the Shreveport chapter of the American Heart Association, my last time with an indoor crowd in the hundreds.

The first paragraph of my comments wasn't anything special, as I realized my speech lacked the striking succinctness of Amy's. That's when I went off-script. What came next wasn't anything historic, but it was a necessary change of pace.

"I'm not a hotel owner. I don't hold a seat on the Chamber of Commerce. I don't have an economic stake in today's issue. I'm a fiancé. I am going to marry a woman who I love very much. And we're very excited. And the thing that we don't have right now is a plan."

Before I knew it, the two-minute tone buzzed my final sentences. As I hung up, my phone lit up with a text from Amy.

"GREAT JOB!!!!!"

The clerk sounded moments later, "Thank you, and that concludes public testimony on this item, Chairman Cox."

The meeting had officially blown past the three-hour mark.

Sup. Desmond added the crucial amendment to the already agreed upon item details.

"It's, I think, appropriate today, particularly with all the speakers talking about weddings and things like that. Today, my beautiful wife, Carrie and I, it's our 36th wedding anniversary. So June is a very popular time for weddings.... At the beginning of the pandemic our public health officials told us the goal was to stabilize our health system, make sure we have enough hospital beds, secure a healthy supply of medical equipment, including ventilators to protect our vulnerable. We've done all that and if you look at our hospital numbers, they have decreased dramatically."

This point would be debated extensively in the discussion to follow, as other supervisors and Dr. Wooten both pointed out the inaccuracies that hospitalizations lagging positive cases might cause.

He concluded, "You know, we've got nightclubs open, and bars, and restaurants, where we don't take names…. I'd like to ask that we send a letter to the governor asking for guidance for the following businesses: wedding receptions, hotel meetings, and conferences, and planned private events."

After a concurrence from Sup. Gaspar, the detractors arrived in force.

First, Sup. Fletcher demurred, "Look, it's no surprise I'm not supportive of this effort. We have now, time and again, gone through this. This drill of sending the governor a letter to demand expedited reopenings…. We put in place these triggers to warn us of significant increases in cases. And we have had the community outbreaks trigger not just Thursday, but we hit it Thursday, and then we hit it Friday. And then we hit it Saturday, and we hit it Sunday, and then we hit it Monday. And my guess is we're going to hit it again today."

Sup. Fletcher was expected to be the "nay" out of the group. However, that's when the conversation turned back to Sup. Jacob, the fence-sitter. If she demurred, would it be enough to sway one of the other two, whom Amy had previously been confident in?

"I've met with some of these groups, and they've done a good job. They make good arguments. And there may well be some inconsistency, but I'm not sure we're in a position to ask the governor for something that locally we cannot approve by the health standards, and what's been laid out by our public health officers."

Desmond responded, after Dr. Wooten had a chance to comment that she was only currently against reopenings during the week to come, until more data was available.

Sup. Desmond pointed out, "As a Boy Scout, I learned 'be prepared,' and so I want to be prepared with this next group of businesses that we're able to open once our numbers get normalized. I'm not asking for them to open. I'm not even asking Dr. Wooten to open them at this point in time until she is satisfied. So, you know, I just want to point out that we're trying, I'm trying, to get local control here sooner rather than later."

The Chief Administrative Officer added, "We have been working closely with many of the callers that were on the phone today, particularly in the events area. And we have gone through their criteria and made some suggestions which they have absolutely put into their protocols…. We just now need to make sure that those guidances get issued and that the circumstances here in San Diego County would allow us to move forward. And that would be Wilma's call at that particular time."

Sup. Jacob nodded.

"If your motion is to ask for guidance and then whatever guidance and whatever we do in the future, we would adhere to our public health officer in terms of moving forward on any of these sectors. I will support your motion."

With a short agreement by Cox, the supervisors' comment period was finally at an end, and looking positive. If they were to vote against the measure today, it would take until the lone-standing July meeting at the earliest before any of this could be resolved. Under a best-case scenario, the governor could very well issue guidance in time for our August wedding to have its guest count (or rather, a guest limit).

The vote for the amendment received a 4-1 result in favor. Now came the final vote for the entire item. After four "aye's" and a single "no," the entire item had passed, just beyond the three-and-a-half-hour mark, around 12:30 p.m.

The clerk reported, "That motion passes with Supervisor Fletcher voting no, although the supervisors being present and voting aye." The seal of San Diego County screen appeared, now with green, red, and blue boxes for yes, no, and abstain, respectively.

"Yes" advanced the motion.

I could finally eat my lunch and celebrate an approval for a request to petition the governor.

8
THE MUSIC STOPS

San Diego, CA – June 23rd, 2020

"CONGRATULATIONS EVERYONE!!!!"

Amy didn't have to go back and add that at the top of her post. It was the first thing she typed into the status bar, just beneath the banner photo of the masked bride and groom.

A feeling of relief washed over her, knowing she had made a first and effective step in her fight, CAPE's goals, and after hearing the other callers on the county meeting, the needs of a swath of sports organizers, street market vendors, and parents too.

"Teamwork makes the dream work! Next step is working with state officials to get the guidelines reviewed by the California Department of Public Health (they are currently reviewing them) and get this pushed up on Newsom's agenda."

It all sounded simple enough. Have the CDPH, with their team of specialists, confirm the guidelines were sufficient. Then, get the guidelines to the governor, and when the light turned green, hit the gas and get back on track.

Realistically, that kind of simplicity hadn't been any part of this pandemic, and certainly hadn't shown its face during the county meeting. When the swing vote, Sup. Jacob, had pushed back against Jim's amendment, Amy's heart had raced and her group text with the CAPE board swarmed like a hornet's nest. Luckily, Jim had nimbly saved the day, specifying that CAPE's ask neither contradicted the board's prior actions, nor did it contradict Dr. Wooten's advice. That had been and would be their goal: let us thread the needle. Just give the industry a fighting chance.

But not everyone felt that way. The subreddit r/SanDiego bemoaned the action that night, as u/player23 bemoaned, "WTF! How can they even think of this, after we just had our worst two-day stretch…all they care about is money."

The post's "O.P.", coincidentally our wedding photographer-to-be, shared his reply from his eponymous account: "They weren't asking for wedding venues to be immediately reopened. The message was distorted by this headline."

In another sign of the times, online vitriol had begun to erupt in this stage of the pandemic. Player23 shot back that the Republican Party was "a death cult," as if that had anything to do with this issue.

For Amy, there wasn't a bottle of champagne that night, or any celebration in particular. Once she'd posted the message to the group, it was a sigh of relief and a feeling that movement was finally underway. She wasn't shouting into a void any longer.

Of all the topics discussed at the county meeting, one rather wise observation had been made during Sup. Jacob's first retort. Since the start of June's business reopenings and protests, cases were climbing, and they were climbing much faster with each passing week.

"I'm really, really concerned, even for the rest of this week, what we're going to be seeing in terms of the outbreaks. And I think we need to watch that very, very carefully and to make sure as we continue, that it is done safely. We don't want to dial back, and that's another fear. If things go bad, then we're not moving forward anymore. We're dialing back."

It would be less than a week later that Jacob would be proven right.

Amy would share, "Just in case you haven't heard, bars, wineries and breweries that do not have a license to serve food will be closing in San Diego County on Wednesday at the latest. The county will also pause all sector reopening efforts until at least August 1, 2020."

***

Chandler, AZ – July 13th, 2020

My suitcase, still waiting to be unpacked, sat in the corner of our bedroom as I worked at the kitchen counter. Kate and I had just returned from a weekend in San Diego, our first since making our move to Arizona. This was our first summer in the Phoenician inferno, so the coastal breezes of San Diego were a welcome reprieve. I greatly missed the coastal air conditioning that morning as my own HVAC system went into overdrive, with outdoor temps climbing toward 109° Fahrenheit.

That pleasant San Diego weather had been critical for Kate's bridal shower, which we hosted in her parents' front yard, with a single in-person attendee from outside the household.

It felt transgressive to be attending my wife's bridal shower, something that I was always under the impression wasn't a place for the groom-to-be. But these were extraordinary circumstances.

I was in charge of drink distribution and adjusting the umbrellas for Kate, her friend, and her mom. My father-in-law-to-be watched from the second story balcony, grinning and sipping on a drink of his own, enjoying some indoor peace and quiet with the rest of us scrambling outdoors.

While Kate's creativity wasn't the reason I married her, it certainly made my top ten. In a few short weeks, she'd pivoted from her meticulously planned bridal shower to a virtual one, aided by her maid of honor. A local artist guided the attendees through a painting lesson, with virtual guests joining from as far away as Fort Worth, Chicago, and Amite City, Louisiana.

In the end, my mee mee had the best painting of the group, a lifelong painter herself.

Kate smiled and laughed throughout, hunching slightly into the webcam's view, playing both honoree and virtual hostess at once. I half expected to see sadness in her eyes, but joy and love were all I could discern as her two long-haired dachshunds, Dusty and Ranger, weaved in and out underneath the card table I'd propped up hours earlier.

This San Diego trip had had a dual purpose, which we fulfilled the day before: signing and pre-filing our marriage certificate.

What was normally a needlessly complicated governmental process was now a needlessly complicated governmental process complicated by government-imposed restrictions.

Almost two months prior to our appointment, Kate and I planned the date and time, during which we'd need to personally appear at the county administration building, and file our certificate, which our officiant would sign the day of our wedding ceremony, and we would then keep.

Kate showed me a list of three dates on her laptop, the only three dates in between COVID's commencement and our wedding, where we'd be able to secure the all-important piece of paper. We picked the second-to-last option, just so that we'd have a fallback option.

If COVID had taught us anything in its first hundred days, it was that a backup plan was never a bad idea.

Although a backup plan doesn't always work. Sometimes it takes a plan "C," plan "D," or even a plan with a letter from the Greek alphabet. The paperwork for my driver's license took me three visits to the DMV when I was sixteen. If I was that unsuccessful a decade later, our wedding day wouldn't be recognized by the state, and we'd lose out on being able to share a joint healthcare account during an ongoing pandemic.

Kate and I started in the county administration parking garage, just off a street named Broadway. It was a short walk up the stairs to surface level, and then a few blocks across Waterfront Park, until we reached the front steps of the large building. That's where we found a tent with masked city employees, who checked for our names, then put us in line for a temperature check.

After fifteen minutes in line, we were inside the administration building, and immediately found ourselves lost again. We made our way to the second floor, where the marriage certificates were processed.

It was another wait in that room full of masked and socially distanced individuals. Most of them had chosen to forego the ceremony madness and just tie the knot right then and there.

With another short wait and a move to the room next door, Kate and I were soon able to depart the admin building with our partially filled and certifiably stamped document, some fifty or sixty dollars poorer.

Afterward, we took some celebratory photos at Waterfront Park. It was there three months before that the CROSS'd Fest had been the source of some of San Diego's earliest community COVID spread, according to the announcement they'd shared to Instagram.

With the bridal shower and marriage certificate accomplished, the last pieces were falling into place. A future that was so in flux had been a challenge to plan around, but with half our guest list backing out at this point, a wedding with 55 invitees wasn't as much of a gamble as 125 had been.

At least, that was the idea, still staring at my suitcase a week later.

My procrastination drifted from thinking about laundry to considering a trip to Twitter. The COVID news on Twitter, which usually featured daily Cuomo or Newsom press conferences, had been a source of either excitement or discomfort as cases rose or waned. Today would be the latter, and the worst in recent memory.

My wish for events guidance suddenly became a monkey's paw.

The governor's Twitter posted, "NEW: #COVID19 cases continue to spread at alarming rates. CA is now closing indoor operations STATEWIDE for: restaurants, wineries, movie theaters, family entertainment, zoos, museums, and cardrooms…Bars must close ALL operations."

Our wedding was already shaping up to be an outdoor gathering. We weren't sure what the liturgically necessary indoor portion would look like, but we assumed it would be heavily reduced at best. Luckily, we had chosen Mary Star of the Sea for its small, intimate nature. A wedding ceremony with the priest, the couple, and their parents wouldn't have looked totally ludicrous, like it might have inside a downtown cathedral.

But that was when my eyes saw the familiar "Show this thread," a feature that had been added to Twitter in lieu of expanding tweets beyond 280 characters from the original 140. The next Tweet was the one that chilled me.

"NEW: As #COVID19 cases and hospitalizations continue to rise, 30 counties will now be required to CLOSE INDOOR OPERATIONS for: fitness centers, places of worship, offices for non-critical sectors, personal care services, hair salons and barbershops, and malls. Counties impacted: Colusa, Contra Costa, Fresno…San Diego."

After seeing Los Angeles earlier in the list and knowing there were only a handful of counties left in the count, I wasn't surprised when San Diego made the list. But it didn't mean for a second that I hadn't hoped the county would be spared.

Putting two-and-two together, this meant that San Diego's Catholic churches were closed indefinitely, besides what they could arrange in outdoor spaces, which few of them had access to.

The soft launch of the tier system had dawned in the state of California, for better or for worse.

In the Governor's press conference for that day, each of California's counties appeared on screen. Obviously, San Francisco and Los Angeles were purple zones, defined as "uncontrolled spread." San Diego too was dark purple, like the worst type of severe thunderstorm on a doppler radar or air quality index.

I could list the bewildering establishments permitted to stay open and operate while places of worship were shuttered, but that didn't do much good before, and it wasn't about to do any good now. The deed was done.

I wanted to be the one to tell Kate, but first I wanted to know our options for celebrating safely, and if there was a chance we'd have any at all. I prayed Kate wouldn't land on that COVID update before I had the chance to make a few calls.

First, I phoned Mary Star of the Sea. While I wasn't breaking the news to them, it was obvious I was one of their first members to ask.

"Uh, we're going to have to check that out," the marriage minister told me. "What we can do is what we've done with Masses. It would be on the elementary school tennis court."

After a quick thank you and a promise to check back soon, I Google-Mapped the Mary Star of the Sea elementary school tennis court, just to confirm it was as I remembered.

The search, and a quick look at the recent Facebook photos, convinced me that a Catholic wedding on this tennis court, which ran along La Jolla's loudest road, and was surrounded by chain link fence, would not be the spiritually fulfilling experience that my fiancée and I had yearned for.

Next, I called Deacon Paul, who had prepared our marriage.

"Hey brother, what's up?"

Paul had been my mentor for years at USC, and knew Kate and I well, guiding us both spiritually through our early years, and even before we knew one another. He had a down-to-earth manner that made him as relatable to the students as he was an excellent preacher to parents, who might be dropping their kids off on their move-in day or visiting for parents' weekend.

Paul had also driven for UPS for decades. Unlike most priests and sisters, Paul's deaconhood was grounded in a blue-collar work ethic, and with a life experience that had brought him face to face with far more than one difficult person. He'd shared many of his stories with me during our sessions of spiritual direction, and with Kate too, during our marriage prep meetings.

Part of Paul's hard work was in his training to be a Deacon, and it showed in his homilies at the Caruso Catholic Center. He did things by the book, because in many ways, he *was* the book. He seemed to have memorized our catechism cover to cover.

"Hey, Paul. You see the COVID update for today?"

"Sorry, just stepped out of a meeting. I can check it out."

I always hesitated to call out of the blue, because I knew Paul would pick up morning, noon, or night. Most of our phone chats ran overtime too, occasionally putting each of our jobs at risk. It sounded like he'd been nice enough to leave a meeting for this call, which was necessary today.

"They're going to close churches. We were thinking the churches would be the next thing to open up, but now it's the opposite. It's all moving in the opposite direction. Mary Star of the Sea is going to look at our options, but they didn't sound good."

"Oh man."

I was hoping I wasn't going to force him to spend time researching, time he should be spending in his meeting, but the loud typing on the other end of the line made it seem like that was already the case. He muttered a few notes, trying to read quickly.

"I'm just about to share it with Kate, and I want her to know our options. I figured we didn't have any—"

"Hey, Rob? I'm gonna look into this. I'm gonna check. No promises, but I'm gonna see."

"Thanks, I really appreciate that."

"Of course, brother."

As soon as Paul had hung up, Amy had already found a moment to call me, completing the informational trifecta.

"Hey, Amy."

"Hey! Wow, that's so unexpected. I'm so sorry."

I paced in the bedroom, trying to keep my voice down as best I could.

"It doesn't seem like this changes the plans for the reception, besides confirming what we already expected."

Amy shook her head. "No, I think the reception still works as a restaurant designation. I can confirm with them today though. They'll probably ask for some more modifications."

"Sure. The church is tough for us though, and that's probably the sticking point. I'm sure you've planned plenty of weddings for plenty of religions. I don't know if we can have a reception if there's no actual marriage that happens. I mean, I know that's kind of old-fashioned."

My voice trailed off as I started to question the strictness of my own beliefs, but Amy didn't let that doubt persist.

"Whatever you two decide, we'll do our best to make it happen. Don't worry."

Amy had planned extravagant events with incredible numbers of moving parts, permits, and celebrities, yet here we were, giving her the challenge of fifty-five people trying to have church and a meal.

"Thanks, Amy."

With the third call complete, I cracked the bedroom door and took a deep breath.

I hadn't had to break bad news to very many people in my life. Still, I've learned a great deal about the right way to breach such things, from parents, high school football coaches, and the like. Whether it was the passing of an extended family member or sharing that a player had suffered a season-ending injury, I'd done my best to absorb their best practices.

"Kate? Can I talk to you in here, when you have a chance?"

She turned and removed an earbud.

"I can take a break. Is something wrong?"

"Yeah."

If she was already asking if something was wrong, I knew I wasn't hiding it very well.

She passed into the bedroom and leaned back on some pillows, while I sat at the foot of the bed, holding one of her knees with as comforting a touch as I could.

"Newsom just announced new rules, and they closed churches. It means they probably won't let us inside."

She frowned.

"Can he do that?"

"I don't know. They just... did it."

"But like, if it was just us and the priest?"

"That's what I'm trying to figure out. It seems like it's nobody now."

"What about, like, ten? Or five?"

It reminded me of Genesis 18, as Abraham pleaded with God not to destroy an entire city so long as enough righteous people remained in it.

"Zero. I'm sorry."

After months of telling Kate everything would be OK, and that we'd figure it all out, it was finally time to discuss the possibility of failure. I couldn't keep up the happy face this time.

She sighed and asked, "What do you think?"

"I called Mary Star of the Sea, and Deacon Paul, and we're going to find out more, but—"

"How soon? Our wedding's in two weeks. We could still do the reception, if they don't ban that, right?"

I thought about it.

"You would want to do a reception without our actual wedding?"

She sighed and looked out the window toward our little stretch overlooking West Pecos Road.

"I don't know."

"I feel like it has to be all or nothing."

She frowned and shrugged.

"But if we can't, then we have to cancel everything. And we're so close."

Planning was off the table now. We needed a miracle.

Kate's initial hunch ended up being right. In February of 2021, the Supreme Court would rule in favor of places of worship:

"[California] says that religious exercises involve (1) large numbers of people mixing from different households; (2) in close physical proximity; (3) for extended periods; (4) with singing…. California errs to the extent it suggests its four factors are always present in worship, or always absent from the other secular activities its regulations allow. Nor has California sought to explain why it cannot address its legitimate concerns with rules short of a total ban. Each of the State's shortcomings are telltale signs this Court has long used to identify laws that fail strict scrutiny."

9
I DO, AT LAST

La Jolla, CA – August 1st, 2020

Most grooms are nervous on the day of their wedding but looking around the back room of our La Jolla venue that Saturday morning, I didn't get the sense that I was the one who was the most nervous.

Instead, it was my groomsmen, little brothers James, Michael, and Joey, my longtime friends, both named Alex, and my father David, who collectively looked pale.

They each would steal a glance at me every so often, wondering if I too was about to vomit or dart.

I wasn't nervous today, at least, not compared to how nervous I had been leading up to today. I was nervous that we wouldn't make it to this point. Today, I was finally where I had hoped and dreamed Kate and I would be. Wedding day nerves didn't hold a stick to that.

For all the bad luck we'd had, the two-and-a-half weeks between July 13th and today featured more than one stroke of good luck.

First, and most importantly, California's resurgence of cases had begun to wane from the moment the tiers soft launched a few weeks prior. The week ending July 11th, 2020 was the peak of the summer case surge in San Diego, and hospitalizations had waned a week or two behind the case peak.

While this didn't mean the coast was clear for August 1st, it also wasn't far off from where we'd been back in June when county guidance was requested: on the mend.

The second stroke of luck, our dream rehearsal dinner site, a restaurant on the bay, became available due to a cancellation. Furthermore, Amy was able to get us

a discount that was within our budget range, and we were given an event we orig-
inally thought would be out of reach, and at one of the places Kate and I had gone
on dates so many times before.

The third and final miracle was courtesy of both Amy and Deacon Paul, who
had been able to tie up loose ends in their respective fields, ensuring that the restaurant classification would hold, and that our marriage would count in the eyes
of the Catholic Church, respectively.

One more setback to any of the above, and we would've had to call it all off.

That's not to say we'd reached August 1st unscathed, either. Our final nuptial
casualties included a dance floor, bouquet toss, and Mary Star of the Sea, all sub-
tracted from the wedding day for pandemic reasons. Our guest list was still surprisingly strong, with at least fifty of the original hundred and twenty-five in at-
tendance. The guests were all temperature checked upon arrival (and would all be
COVID-free in the weeks to follow).

Fifty proved to be a nice number, and one that was enjoyably more intimate
than the original roster might have been. Whereas most brides spend the entire
cocktail hour walking table to table, we were able to do two socially distanced laps
instead.

In the groom's chambers, my dad still wouldn't stop looking at me with wide
eyes, the look that I assume every groom gets the morning of their wedding, half
expecting that I might do something unexpected.

"You ready?" he asked for the third time since I'd arrived moments earlier,
riding in a green sports car convertible getaway car we'd rented.

"Oh yeah."

"Good!"

I grinned.

"You keep asking me that."

He shrugged.

"Don't want you to change your mind."

That wasn't going to happen. At this point, they'd need to force me out of here
in handcuffs, not that that wasn't still a possibility. I still worried a Christmas

Vacation-esque SWAT team might hop the hedgerow halfway through our homily.

I'd gotten the same careful treatment from Amy the night before. Just after the rehearsal dinner, she'd called me with the final details, adding her sage warning to all grooms: "Don't be hungover on your wedding day."

That scared me straight. One of the groomsmen proceeded to gift me a bottle of Angel's Envy Bourbon, which went almost untouched during our game of Catan that night.

Almost.

Amy had texted me an hour after I'd woken up too, holding a mug that read "YOU GOT THIS."

The pandemic-proof outdoor Irish step dancing class outside our La Jolla Airbnb rang in my ears as I grinned and nodded, texting back, "The groom is of sound mind and body! One less thing to worry about."

Now, Amy was in her final form. Throughout the afternoon and evening, she very well could be mistaken for a guest of the wedding, were you not watching closely enough to see her as she expertly orchestrated each and every facet of the day.

Her sequined mask was the first thing I could see as she poked her head through the door of the groom's suite.

"It's time!"

I nodded and gave my dad one more look before we stepped out the door.

"I'm still ready."

"Good!"

He smiled and patted me on the shoulder for the fourth time.

The walk from the groom's suite to the side lawn isn't a long one on paper, but in the effort to keep me from spotting Kate, Amy led the group of men through a labyrinth, with the occasional smile and greeting given to attendees freshly arrived, searching for the restrooms.

After my Apple Watch detected that I'd been walking enough to potentially register a workout, we'd reached the south lawn of the building, which is surrounded on three sides by hedges. The venue allowed events to use any of these areas in addition to their spacious ballroom. Today, we'd use all three. The indoor ballroom would remain mostly untouched, by comparison.

This south yard would be where photos would take place after the ceremony, and where the two parties would await their walk down the aisle. The north lawn would host the cocktail hour during additional photo taking, and the front area would host the ceremony and dinner, under rows of palm trees and a sprawling oak.

Amy handed me off to Deacon Paul, who gripped my shoulder securely, akin to a quarterback ensuring a football won't be fumbled as the play gets underway.

"Thanks, Amy."

She smiled, "Remember, don't walk too fast."

"I got it."

Turning to Paul, finally there was someone who wasn't worried that I'd dart during the nuptials.

He grinned, "Alright, Smatty. You ready?"

"She told me not to walk too fast, but we won't have to worry about that."

Paul laughed. He'd had to force me to slow down my processional walk on more than one occasion at the Caruso Catholic Center, where I'd altar served for him many times.

"Let's go ahead and bow, and I'll do a blessing."

I bowed and closed my eyes, Paul prayed one final blessing over me.

Ever since I'd phoned him that Monday morning in July, Paul had been there at every step of the way.

Within the week, he had secured a dispensation from the parish and the diocese that permitted us to marry, despite our not being inside Mary Star of the Sea, or even on its tennis court. When he'd phoned me with the news, I'd been floored.

He'd told Kate and me more than once, and would add during his homily, "You know how special you two are? I think you're the first Catholics to get a destination wedding since the Kennedys."

I didn't doubt it.

It was a strange occurrence. Here we were so focused on the church and the religious rite that we were accepting the outdoor ceremony, while other brides and grooms had pulled every trick in the book, always foiled by our infallible Pope and forced back indoors.

I even thought back (way back) to the chat Paul and I'd had at Blaze Pizza on Figueroa four years before, when I'd disclosed that, despite my eagerness to date Kate, I feared she was too mature, and on and on.

Paul almost slapped me, and certainly knocked sense into me metaphorically.

"Don't do that. You're right for each other."

And that was that.

As Paul's blessing concluded and I motioned the sign of the cross, I tried to hide the fact that I'd been stuck in my own head when I was supposed to be listening to his prayer.

As the music began to echo around the lawn areas, a hush came over the groomsmen in tow. I made my way under the venue's oak tree and toward the back of the rows of gorgeous golden wood chairs, which Aunt Fernanda had helped secure for us. As I began to walk, I did end up moving at a faster pace than I'd promised Amy moments prior.

You never really know who to look at when a crowd is facing you, but I did my best to nod and make eye contact with everyone to my right and left. James and Fern, Don and Jeannie, whoever was on the outer edges of each row. And maybe one double take, spotting someone you thought would back out at the last moment, there in full force, and with a Bed, Bath, and Beyond gift card freshly dropped on the gifts table.

Based on who had sat with whom, I already had a good feeling that Kate and I had properly arranged their seating for the reception to come, as painstaking as that process had been, especially with RSVPs in flux up until the morning of the wedding, when a head cold had eliminated one last attendee.

Paul gestured to the center of the aisle, where I took my place and turned to face the crowd, continuing to nod and smile, now for a whole new row and a half. Luckily, it was time for the coupled groomsmen and bridesmaids to make their way down the aisle.

As I watched each brother, friend, and soon-to-be in-law make their way toward me, lining up to my right and left, I thought back to the many weddings I'd filmed during college, one of which happened to be for Paul's daughter.

But it was another wedding I thought back on at this moment. That groom was a tough guy, having been rostered with an NFL team after a successful college career playing offensive line for an Ivy League team. He and his brothers, whom I'd had the chance to play football with in high school, even towered over those of above-average height like myself.

Despite all his toughness, on the morning of his wedding that groom had cried, not to mention during his ceremony at Fort Worth's St. Patrick's Cathedral, and during the speeches thereafter.

Watching him that morning, I wondered if I would cry as much as he had on the most important day of our respective lives. I hadn't so far.

James, my oldest brother, made his way down the aisle last, giving me a thumbs up, confirming he had the wedding bands secured in his pocket.

The first entry tune faded into the bride's entry, and every eye on the lawn turned to just left of the giant tree, where Doug led Kate into full view of each and every one of us. Kate smiled and Doug maintained a stoic focus as he ensured his daughter wouldn't trip on a cobblestone or sink a heel into the soil.

Kate smiled as our eyes locked. She was beautiful, and her dress was just as astonishing. I was floored, not only at how pretty she was, but at how a moment we'd played in our heads for years, which had started to fade in the past two weeks, was actually, finally happening.

And that was when I started to cry.

10
BLOOD RED

San Diego County Admin. Center – August 31st, 2020

Two.

Since the beginning of the pandemic, Amy had successfully planned two weddings. As it stood now, only that number had remained between now and the new year.

So, optimistically, four. Four weddings out of eighty-plus.

Despite case numbers declining dramatically in July, Sacramento was steadfast: California did not believe now was the moment to loosen restrictions.

On August 28th, the administration had announced that the state would incorporate a "Blueprint for a Safer Economy," dubbed the "tier system." Amy had read the release word for word, despite its lengthy nature:

"CDPH will assess indicators weekly on Mondays and release updated tier assignments on Tuesdays.

A county must remain in a tier for a minimum of three weeks before being able to advance to a less restrictive tier.

A county can only move forward one tier at a time, even if metrics qualify for a more advanced tier."

The math wasn't hard. Assuming San Diego County started in anything less than the least restrictive tier—which wasn't likely for a population over three million—it would be up to nine weeks, over two months, until the county would see anything close to a traditional wedding again.

The color coding carried over from the July 13th announcement, akin to a project that was already underway at the time, but not complete enough to match rising case numbers, which had peaked shortly thereafter and declined since.

A chart showed allowances underneath each tier. Paragraphs upon paragraphs further underneath specified further guidelines, linking to a network of publicly accessible PDF files and data.

For all that the CDPH site had to offer on the tier system, each additional word ratcheted control a measure tighter. The devil, it seemed, really was in the details, especially as one kept reading.

"Your county can make tighter restrictions through the local health department, but it cannot loosen them."

The fear of losing local control that Sup. Desmond had argued for on June 23rd had come home to roost. San Diego County still had local control, but only in one direction.

These thoughts coursed through Amy's mind as she watched Desmond cross in front of her, headed to a podium that faced cameras and a socially distanced crowd. They were back on the steps of the County Administration Building, prepared for a new fight.

Around Amy stood her colleagues, each holding the signs from the empty events rally a few weeks earlier and lining the steps behind the podium.

Jim wore his signature tie and button-down shirt, without a jacket, and lowered his face covering, which conveniently collapsed around his neck.

Calling out the names of local business owners, he stumbled over a few of them, among them Tony Amalasteri, owner of a popular pizza joint. But no name gave Jim as much trouble as Amy's.

"Founder of the San Diego Event Coalition, Ellen Daniels, and Amy…"

Laughter rumbled through the group.

"…Ol' cat. Oh no, I'm gonna get it right."

The laughter grew as Amy grinned.

"Amy, Ulkuten. Uklu… Ulkutek… Ul-, I'm sorry Amy."

"You got it," Amy cheered from behind him.

"Ulkutekin!" Jim cheered, like an elementary schooler learning the value of reading syllable by syllable.

"Thank you, Amy."

"You know," he continued, regaining his composure, "while some certain businesses were able to open today, many others continue to be greatly limited and hampered, or even closed. And the announcement from the governor was not enough. The state continues to change the targets and move the goalposts. And in doing so, unfortunately, picking winners and losers."

Jim was electric, and while his logic was usually compelling, his pathos shone more brightly today for the first time since Amy had begun her work with him so many weeks before. Even the most fearful of pandemic positions wouldn't negate Jim's logic: it wasn't whether COVID was a threat or not, but instead how the gray areas had been handled. It was about fair treatment, and it was about acknowledgement that went beyond "hang in there a little bit longer."

Every "turning a corner" or "light at the end of the tunnel" was another stinging insult to this industry, who had been dealt empty words ever since Amy's May comments on Sup. Fletcher's video update.

"All these businesses that are here today are willing to open safely. They all know the safety parameters. They're willing to go above and beyond and meet the safety requirements…. On Friday, we heard about the color codes and the different phrases in the different phases that really don't mean a lot to anybody out there who's not working today. We've heard for so long that what's essential and what's non-essential for many of the people here today, they're labeled non-essential, but they are essential. Putting food on the family's table is essential. Paying a mortgage is essential. Paying rent is essential. Trying to make a living is also essential."

The crowd cheered as Jim invited the first speaker to the stage, proud that for once, they would be heard.

It wasn't just business that had occupied Amy's thoughts during the past month though. In addition to CAPE's goals, Amy also wished to see E.J. and Ariana back in school. They had been affected by the April and May restrictions, and while Amy was happy they hadn't caught COVID at the time, the newest data didn't worry her as much. Other parents felt the same, while still others felt differently. There were pros and cons on all sides, and for that reason, it was one of many topics she'd tried to avoid in conversation, even though everyone wanted to talk about it.

A path for exiting a pandemic wasn't something any rational person opposed, but the summer surge had been a wake-up call. It was a moment of divergence, if nothing else. COVID didn't end with the first outbreak, and seemed like it was capable of mutating.

For that reason, it might not ever go away. Not until there was a vaccine available, at least.

The tier system certainly wouldn't disappear anytime soon either, with how much work had been devoted to the program.

Amy, CAPE, and the San Diego Events Coalition weren't about to sit around and do nothing, whether they were on the front steps of the admin building, or in its backyard. On August 10th and 12th, Amy posted to the SD Events for the first time since the tiers had struck in July.

"The San Diego Event Coalition will be hosting an Empty Event Rally this Thursday at 2pm at Waterfront Park…to ask for further support until we are able to reopen."

"Further support" included asking for additional unemployment benefits, PPP programs specific to event industry members, and involvement in local and state reopening planning.

"[There will be] 48 tables with 480 empty chairs. Each table represents 250,000 unemployed event industry workers nationwide. These are the florists, audio techs, caterers, planners, venue managers and entertainers that have worked tirelessly to bring you years of amazing memories…. Tomorrow we stand six feet apart…but we stand together to ask for assistance."

The irony wasn't lost on Amy that she was now co-planning a non-event on the very grounds where the CROSS'd Fest had taken place only six months prior, and near the building where some of her own clients had, or would, wait in line to elope and forgo their planned ceremony, and her services along with them.

With a microphone in front of the Guardian of Water Statue, the emcee that day had roared, "If you are an event professional, I want you to make your voice heard right now. Come on, let's make it heard!"

Hundreds of attendees, all socially distanced, stood on the sidewalk between Waterfront and the coastline. Their cheers were drowned out only by the industry's fleet of box trucks that had momentarily stopped traffic, blaring their horns as loudly as they could.

Between the attendees and the emcee stood the promised 48 tables and 480 empty chairs. Each chair and table sported a different poster, banner, or sign in SDEC and CAPE's signature colors:

"PRODUCTION ASSISTANT NOT ALLOWED TO WORK."

"LIVE EVENT STAGE MANAGER. UNEMPLOYED."

"EVENTS ARE MOMENTS. EVENTS ARE MEMORIES. EVENTS ARE LIVELIHOODS."

"Twelve million people are unemployed from the events industry, making up thirty-three percent...of the unemployed nationwide. Our industry was the first to be shut down, and it will be the last to be reopened because of the impact of COVID-19!"

The head of San Diego Pride took the mic next, and shared, "With the current moratorium on special events, our LGBTQ community members have been left without a way to safely gather. Many youth and seniors in our community have been forced to quarantine with unsupportive family members. For the first time in over 45 years, we have not been able to celebrate Pride in person this past July.... Keep our dedicated staff employed, keep our thousands of volunteers engaged in community service, and be here for San Diego to celebrate Pride when it is time to do so safely, once again."

The emcee took the stage again, pointing toward the trucks lining the street.

"These are the empty trucks of the San Diego event businesses, traditionally filled to the brim with equipment, staff, and everything necessary to make magical venues come to life, and then clean up afterwards. These trucks are now empty.

They will stay empty until public officials let us know it's safe to hold events again."

The horns blared again in protest, leading the group on a march around the administration building.

It was a trucker protest of sorts, and a full year before such an event had taken on a negative connotation in the Great White North.

The non-event had felt good, as Amy had stood arm-in-socially-distanced-arm with her fellow event professionals, lowering her mask only for a few seconds so that the crowd could acknowledge the group of twenty who had organized it.

But the bleeding had already begun, and a few regional news stories and social media hits couldn't stop it.

In Washington D.C., and across the country, other empty event rallies had happened. But in California, there was something unique about the work of these groups. Event professionals in neighboring states and countries weren't suffering. They were benefitting, to some extent, from the runaway business that had fled more restrictive states. Those Betches Brides polls had actually come to fruition for them.

Amy had asked on Facebook, "How is everyone dealing with postponements for a 2nd or 3rd time? … As a planner I have to move all their contracts, which is hours of work, and some of them booked at my rate from more than a year ago."

Another planner had replied, "I try to see the clients' perspective on their day being canceled twice. I have a bunch of people who canceled and have no new date yet, so if they start pushing into 2022 then I gotta do something."

On the ABC 10 live cast of the press conference, a chyron scrolled through all the businesses that were given new permissions as of September 2020, among them places of worship, museums, restaurants, hair and nail salons, and gyms.

The next event speaker, Ellen, snapped Amy into the present again, as her moving speech about her children and her struggling business had brought tears to their eyes.

"A little emotional there!" she admitted, as the crowd applauded to encourage her.

"I'd like to invite Amy, an amazing colleague, who's been in this fight with me from the start."

Amy made her way down the steps and to the podium, already chomping at the bit to speak for the first time since the board meeting. Today, she wouldn't be limited by a tone that buzzed her after two minutes, nor would she be forced to comment by phone. Today, Amy could let the public and state officials know how she, and those around her, really felt.

"Events are literally illegal. And my job is literally illegal. I have two small children. I can't provide for them."

Having seen her share of speeches at weddings, most of them casual, a few of them drunken, and all of them heartfelt, Amy toed a different line, one of abject—albeit restrained and professional—indignation.

"A 'gathering' is two or more people outside of a household. Yet you can go to a restaurant, you can dine with hundreds of other people. You have no idea who they are. Yet you can't get forty to fifty people together…. We can contact trace. We can test prior to these gatherings. And yet they're still not allowed. In fact, events are not even a dropdown or an industry on the state's guidelines."

Yet the chyron still scrolling at the bottom of the screen already said as much. Nowhere in the state plans were the unemployed event professionals even named.

"How is that? I mean, you look, it says convention centers and festivals. No venues. No reception halls. Nothing…. Myself and a group of our colleagues, we created the California Association for Private Events and we drafted guidelines, you know, fifteen pages of very well thought out guidelines that we ran through the county reopening team. We ran through Dr. Wooten, and they sent out to California and Sacramento. And unfortunately, it fell on deaf ears."

The barrage didn't cease. Amy's stressed eyes glared into the crowd, sharing a laundry list of unsanctioned parties, swap meets, and street festivals that were allowed to go about as they wished, because the state only enforced the rules against those who acted within the law.

"As a billion-dollar industry in California, we're unable to provide for our families, which is absolutely ludicrous given that we're essentially taking the guidelines that are already pre-approved and asking to operate under there."

And that was that. With a curt thank you to Sup. Desmond, Amy replaced her mask and stepped aside.

She took a breath for what felt like the first time in minutes.

As Jim made his closing remarks, as Amy shook hands after the event, and as she drove home that evening with all these thoughts swirling in her mind, one thought stood at the center of it all: she finally felt activated. And she liked it.

The next day, numerous venues around San Diego would light up red for Save Events Day, including the historic Del Mar Fairgrounds.

The red not only signified the danger of empty venues. It matched the color returning to Amy's blood. It was time to take this fight to the next level.

11
ONE BLOCK AWAY

Sacramento, CA – September 8th, 2020

Kevin Gordon worked so closely to the capitol that he could practically reach out and touch it. At the corner of "L" Street and Tenth, his office gave him a full view of the front steps, the mall, almost all of it. It was a view he'd worked his whole life to appreciate, and one that made him proud.

Kevin's office neighbored government offices, legal firms, and even the local NPR affiliate, KQED, but his profession didn't fall under law or media. He had a 24/7 eye on Sacramento for a reason, and that was because he was a lobbyist.

When it came to telling people what he did for a living, Kevin would choose his words carefully, acknowledging that the term "lobbyist" is sometimes regarded as a dirty word, both in government and to the public. And when Kevin did reveal his occupation, people proved to be as quick to misunderstand as they were slow to re-educate themselves.

What many didn't realize is that there is more than one kind of lobbyist, at least by Kevin's estimation. Whereas many of his colleagues were special interest lobbyists—and damn good ones at that—Kevin was a public interest advocate. He was a lobbyist who represented public schools, parents, and students, not to mention a massive roster of other groups that needed his help accessing the increasingly insulated halls of Sacramento.

Though, there was a time when Sacramento wasn't so hard to break into and thank goodness for that.

Lobbying wasn't what Kevin thought he'd do for a living, nor did he think he'd be the co-founder of an entire firm like Capitol Advisors. But here he was, celebrating the firm's eighth anniversary just the year prior. While Capitol Advisors had plenty of partners with more traditional paths into the public advocacy sector, including former state superintendent Jack O'Connell, Kevin first stumbled into the arena almost by accident.

His origin was one of those late 20th century American success stories that is rare now, especially in the age of social media ubiquity and a post-9/11 security state. Always drawn to the hustle and bustle of the capitol building, as a young man, Kevin found himself in the corridors of the capitol on a sunny day in the 1970s, the day that Robert Rishell's portrait of outgoing Governor Ronald Reagan would be hung in the capitol.

Spotting a scrum of reporters with an array of TV cameras set to capture the important event, Kevin inquired with one of the correspondents about what was happening and got invited to join the line-up of reporters who would be able to ask questions. Moments after the formalities of the ceremony, he got his turn to visit with both "the Gipper" and a young Jerry Brown, who himself would embark on not one, but two California governorships, spanning sixteen years over five decades.

The rest, as they say, is history (after Kevin had managed to gain a handful of advanced degrees from the esteemed UC system and the University of San Francisco, of course).

Public advocacy got off to a quick start for the firm as the chief lobbyist for the California School Boards Association. An important milestone was his early success in 1994, when he stewarded the passage of SB-2005, which guaranteed that those convicted of drug and sex offenses involving a minor would be barred from teaching in the public school system, even after serving a sentence. It read:

"An act to amend Section 44425 of the Education Code, relating to teacher credentialing.

Existing law requires the Commission on Teacher Credentialing to revoke the credential of any person convicted of any sex offense or controlled substance offense, as defined, when the conviction becomes final or imposition of sentence is suspended.

This bill, in addition, would provide that the revocation is final without possibility of reinstatement of the credential if the conviction is for specified sex offenses or for controlled substance offenses in which an element of the controlled substance offense is distribution to, or use by, a minor."

SB-2005 was a gargantuan effort, which was a surprise to some who might think the legislation a no-brainer. Kevin certainly had, before his conversations with the teachers' unions and others in the legislature. What was so consequential about emboldening the sacred bond between children and those in their classrooms?

But that was a public advocate's daily struggle: convince the brainiest in government to trust their gut, and of course, to listen to their constituents over the talking heads on the news and special interest groups knocking at their office doors.

The job was also a two-way road, as Kevin was equally familiar with legislators seeking him out to find out what constituents wanted, or to ask what the law might allow. These were the relationships that formed the bread and butter of any successful lobbying firm, especially Capitol Advisors.

Kevin had a relationship working with governors across seven administrations dating back to that first term of Jerry Brown's. The Newsom administration was off to as great a start as the others, supporting key investments in areas that had been lobbied by Kevin for years, and blessed by surging revenues.

Among many areas of mutual interest to the governor and Kevin's school clients was the notion of providing meals to all kids, rather than limiting good nutrition in schools to those who qualified for free and reduced-cost meals.

Kevin worked with Newsom and his staff to advance investments in teacher development, education funding, school nutrition and student mental health. The success in establishing a universal meals policy was, without question, one of the great results of good policy and advocacy.

That effort only took forty years to get put in writing, but that was just how these things went sometimes. Better late than never, right?

The pandemic had been a different beast entirely, and one in which the span of decades wouldn't be an acceptable timetable for what Kevin's clients asked of him. Moreover, Kevin's clients weren't just parents, children, or school systems anymore. Capitol Advisors had recently signed the California Association for Private Events, and their members, board, and president.

Amy had found Kevin thanks to a parent at a school board meeting, which had become yet another pandemic hotbed of newfound citizen engagement.

Kevin wouldn't soon forget his first chat with Amy, weeks prior. Usually, he's the one to help a client steer their messaging or prepare to speak with legislators. Amy was an informational artillery cannon already loaded, and she just needed to know where to aim.

"We have members in almost all of California's legislative districts," she'd said. "Once we have a message to take to the legislature, I can make sure we've got a coordinated effort that they can individually take to their representatives."

Kevin was gobsmacked. That's the kind of thing that people on his end usually struggle to do, much less someone with no knowledge of what it takes to enact legislative change. To have Amy both harness the resources and know that it was a necessary step made Kevin realize that this client's mission wasn't the only thing out of the ordinary.

There was more than just Amy's smarts, from a strategic perspective. While Kevin felt his firm was the best choice for Amy or anyone else, he couldn't deny that there were other options out there. Truthfully, Amy could have interviewed ten or fifteen other firms before Capitol Advisors.

Instead, Kevin was glad Amy had chosen a public advocacy firm. CAPE's event professionals weren't chasing after the special interest groups, which had plenty of experience with the gyms, restaurants, and other surviving industries Amy's allies had so envied. Rather, CAPE's message was one of public advocacy, just like so many of California's school systems.

And today, CAPE would be listened to at the state level.

Video chat had been a boon for Kevin's line of work, if only the tasks at hand weren't leagues harder to accomplish in the age of COVID. The app bubble began to bounce at the edge of Kevin's screen as he prepared for his next meeting with the CAPE board.

For weeks, Kevin had been working on their behalf to string together a network of lawmakers and administration contacts who would be receptive to their cause. Especially now that the new school year was underway, Kevin could devote time and resources to CAPE, nevertheless continuing to juggle the continued concerns about stimulus money tied up in November's election cycle.

Getting members of the legislature on the same page was hard, but there's strength in numbers, and Kevin had been seeding and germinating such a coterie.

In addition to knowing who CAPE needed to contact at the state level, Kevin was the mind behind the question of "How?" How does one send an email that doesn't get deleted? How does one professionally communicate a sense of urgency to their recipient? And how does one do that between both executive and legislative branches, in tandem?

The best email started with a brief background of Capitol Advisors, which concealed a not-so-hidden connection to the recipient. If Kevin was emailing a senator, for instance, he might point out one of the school districts that he advocated on behalf of was located in their district:

"We are writing in an effort to help the California Association of Private Events (CAPE) on COVID impacts to their very broad-based industry that includes the hospitality industry, major event venues, florists, wedding event businesses, caterers, restaurants and many more."

Once legitimacy and familiarity were established, the email structure plunged headfirst into action, especially projecting inertia that might exist in the other branch of the bicameral state legislature. If Kevin could link a cause back to someone important in the governor's office, that was even better.

He especially liked "my client has had good exchanges" with so and so, a phrase which made it into a non-zero number of his many missives.

Just like advertisers trying to attract young people to their product, so too, Kevin hoped that a senator or assembly member might develop a case of "FOMO," and want to join in a "good exchange" of their own, if only to see what the buzz was about. Others fostered mutual respect for important members of the executive branch, and that motivation frequently proved to be just as effective.

Once he'd laid out the client's need—in CAPE's case, having a seat at the table—it was time for the grand finale:

"The client is clear on the fact that continuing to work with the administration is very important to their cause, but they also want to make sure that the highest-level policy makers on the issue know that they are prepared to share ideas on the criteria."

A sentence like that is what a public advocate lobbyist does best: take the broad desire for government access, specify the ask to the recipient, and then make the client sound like a seasoned veteran and let them speak their truth.

That message, and others, had been more than enough to land a few meetings for Amy and CAPE, including today's meeting with the CDPH.

Amy had added quite a bit to this letter and the others too. Her attention to detail was incredible and exceeded what Kevin might expect from even the most experienced in and around Sacramento.

Except for the governor, of course. Gavin Newsom's detail-oriented demeanor was the stuff of legend. Kevin couldn't think of anyone with more dedication to the details.

The joke went that, in comparison to the meager scraps that Jerry Brown offered, Newsom was an all-you-can-eat buffet. The man rarely minced words or information. For all their similarities, getting Amy and the governor on the same page would be no simple task.

Amy appeared on screen with a few other board members tuning in across the screen.

"Hello, everyone."

"Hi, Kevin," Amy answered.

"Let me know when any of us should jump in."

"You know I will."

Kevin grinned, very much looking forward to another chance to make a difference.

"I'd tell you what to talk about, but you usually come up with something better!"

Amy laughed humbly.

"We'll do our best."

As the administration members entered the digital room, Kevin metaphorically lit the fuse, turned around, and plugged his fingers into his ears, clenching his jaw in preparation for the concussive blast that would soon echo across the street, as an artillery shell of pure persuasion struck home.

***

The hardest part of lobbying, even tougher than the long hours, press tours, and pathological liars, was inaction.

It wasn't hard to see the temptation in the faces of their CDPH meeting partners, as the health officials considered their options in the matter. One of those options, undoubtedly, is to do nothing.

But Kevin wasn't so heartless that he couldn't comprehend the rationale for such inaction. When someone in a position of power makes a choice of any kind, they're on the hook for it. Whether it's voters, party leadership, or the media, when you make a decision in politics, there's odds that the decision will work in your favor just as much as there are odds that it won't. When it doesn't go as planned, the results can be career-ending.

So when one opts to do nothing, or suggests that they're waiting on more guidance, it can be their safest bet.

No one will ever say it to your face, but after years of this work, Kevin knew what a punt looked like when he saw one. Luckily, when Amy returned the proverbial talking stick, Kevin had done his best to prevent that punt from taking place, if only to keep the conversation alive for another week, another meeting, whatever it took.

COVID cases were continuing to decline, and it was now or never for CAPE to gain the administrative access they needed. When the politicians had logged off the call, promising to circle back with Kevin, rather than give him the cold shoulder, he was able to speak candidly.

"Another good step in the right direction, I think."

Amy nodded, taking a drink of water after all the speaking she'd done. The board collectively relaxed their postures too.

"Is this where you think we'll get some action from them?" she asked.

Kevin laughed. If he could predict when a legislature or bureaucracy was ready to act on something, he'd go buy a lotto ticket and predict those numbers too.

"I'm sorry. I do think we're close! I wish I could be more specific than that. I'm going to stick with it."

Amy smiled.

"I understand totally, Kevin. Thanks for all your help."

With that, the call was over, and it was finally time for an afternoon cup of coffee.

As Kevin stood from his desk and checked his calendar for the rest of the day, he couldn't help but glance at the dwindling number of days until the November 3rd election.

He hoped that they were able to make some progress on CAPE's behalf by then, before administrative turnover led to more delay. If something didn't happen soon, there would be no telling what kind of salvo Amy might muster.

Kevin would continue to advise patience, as he did with his other clients. At the same time, he fully understood that the events industry might not have the capacity to wait. They very well could be planning another more accelerated strategy at this moment.

Only able to control his own tactics, Kevin would have to wash his hands of whatever CAPE chose to do outside of that purview. But that wouldn't keep him from eagerly watching out his window, should figurative fireworks erupt outside the capitol building.

12

RESILIENCY

San Diego, CA – September 29th, 2020

Gary sighed, staring at the draft of an email he'd meticulously prepared that morning. Today, San Diego's County Chief Resilience Officer was working from his office in Kearny Mesa, but he had crisscrossed the entire county in the months since the dawn of COVID.

He wanted to provide good news without overpromising, as he knew so many others might have done with so many of their constituents. Realistically, there was good news to share: San Diego's Health Department had heard the email campaign from the events industry loud and clear and would do something about it.

"Amy, I wanted to inform you that Dr Wooten has requested a meeting with the State Public Health Officer regarding events. I am not sure when that meeting will go, hoping over the weekend or early next week."

Gary smirked at the mention of "weekend," as if there was any way to differentiate days of the week when he was running consecutive seven-day workweeks.

"I am pressing at all levels for the State and County to consider developing reopening guidance for wedding receptions – much like State recently did for outdoor playgrounds. I believe that such an opportunity would clearly indicate that the events industry can do such events well and safely...and it would be a 'pilot' for other events."

Gary's advocacy on behalf of events was only his latest effort. After thirty years in the U.S. Marine Corps, finishing with the rank of Colonel, Gary thought he'd seen everything, having served his nation in combat, humanitarian crises, and for incidents for which he'd been sworn to secrecy.

But he wasn't prepared for COVID. At least, not at first, when the call had come from the Miramar Marine Base seven months before.

"A Federal Incident Management Team is being dispatched to the base," Gary's boss had told the county EMS staff at their all-hands meeting that day.

First it was inbound Chinese nationals, but that was soon followed by a cruise ship making an emergency landing in Los Angeles Harbor. Hundreds and thousands of people required pandemic-safe shelter and medical treatment, and they were on a collision course with the Marine base in Gary's backyard.

"We've never done anything like this," one of the other staff groaned, to agreement from the others to Gary's right and left.

Gary chose that moment to speak up, knowing it might be his final moment of peace before a tidal wave overtook his every waking moment.

"Actually, I think we might."

Every head in the room turned toward him. As recently as 2019, Gary had served as the Deputy Commander of every Marine Installation west of the Mississippi. His counterparts collectively remembered that he might just be the man for this job too.

"We have an after-action report from 2014, about the county Hepatitis outbreak."

Whether or not he'd realized as much, Gary's job as head of San Diego's COVID task force began in that instant. And that Hep A report quickly became a boon to San Diego's first days of pandemic preparedness.

Gary was soon returning to his old post at MCAS Miramar, where he would be reunited with old friends, all confronted with a challenge that exceeded anything they'd encountered in the Middle East or South China Sea.

But then, as "the curve" flattened in the weeks and months that followed, there was an even more challenging issue on the horizon: a socioeconomic question. And more than one.

It was around that time that Gary first met Amy, not to mention a swath of small business owners, school superintendents, and so, so many others. As the guidance came from the state, Gary would roll up his sleeves and meet the moment, finding the clearest and most concise way to ferry such information to those it affected in his county and others too. Then, he'd volley their replies and questions to anyone who might listen.

It was Mondays in closed fitness centers, Tuesdays at socially distanced sports complexes, Wednesdays at gutted golf courses, Thursdays on shuttered school playgrounds, weekends in barren places of worship, and so on. Always asking questions and doing everything in his power to help, Gary's efforts had begun to make a difference. Youth sports was one of the first successes he was able to restore to San Diego.

Gary took a Swiss Army Knife approach to problem solving, thanks to his education in the Marine Corps. As that Swiss Army Knife, he tried to juggle it all, except understanding. Gary made it a point never to tell someone, Amy especially, that he understood. Because he didn't. And people were frustrated at being told that their elected officials did understand them.

In truth, no one could but they themselves.

Instead, Gary offered his appreciation, as much on behalf of socioeconomic causes as public health causes. And if there was a tie, he always sided with public health, thanks to the continued advice of Dr. Wooten and her staff.

Gary had such appreciation for the events industry, and slightly more than he might have had for the others, because his own daughter was slated to marry in a few short weeks. If his own family was undergoing challenges with her event, he knew those employed by the industry were even more urgently affected.

This was why his wording had to be perfect in his email to Amy, and the other industry members too.

"I have no idea what the result will be on a renewed push on this topic. I frankly would prepare for the worst, that the state will continue to say 'no' to events and this stance could go into the next calendar year (when a vaccine is available).

Don't give up the fight, Amy.

Semper Fidelis."

***

San Diego, CA – September 30th, 2020

CAPE's "core four" board members had met more times than they could count and included industry leaders from both San Diego and Los Angeles.

Los Angeles debuted in the purple tier a month prior, and while San Diego had some hope for a short recovery, the Angelenos would be three weeks behind, if not further.

"I'm sorry. I only have what I last shared to the Facebook group. I wish they'd gotten back to us by now," explained Amy's fellow San Diegan, who had tried again to make headway with NACE, as Amy had back in the Spring.

"It hasn't been that long," one of the Angelenos offered.

"CDPH could still be working on a plan."

Amy shrugged.

"Maybe. I just don't know how else to get their attention at this point. The lobbying I think is great and continues to get us different contacts. But they're all so focused on re-elections for the next month, I'm worried any momentum we make in October..."

There was a pregnant pause as Amy's voice trailed off.

This core four call was a hard one to be having. Almost a full month after their biggest moves, the group was again low on ideas, and more importantly, lower on funding.

It was almost a laugh to think that only three months earlier, their biggest hurdle was the San Diego Board of Supervisors. Now, the county was one of their most loyal allies, yet they were somehow worse off as summer turned to fall.

What had they gained playing this game by the rules, especially when so many others had shirked guidelines, and even incorporated fines as a cost of doing business?

Maybe it was human nature or survival instincts kicking in, but with their backs against the wall, one of the board members sighed and spoke in a more aggressive tone than normal.

"I'm so fed up with this state crap, I'm ready to dress up in a tux and march on the capitol myself! Maybe that would get their attention."

They laughed. The mental image of the board member picketing in a tux was such a dysfunctional thought.

It was a moment of levity, and that's what they'd needed as much as new ideas. Whatever better thought-out idea they came up with, at least they'd have the dress and tuxedo protest idea to fall back on.

After a few more silly ideas got pitched, and the group had the time to wish each other farewell, Amy hung up.

Typically, as she went into her next work tasks, cooked dinner for the family, and checked how much laundry needed to be done, Amy was able to move on, and let ideas sit in the back of her mind.

But not tonight.

One thought stood solely at the forefront of her headspace as minutes turned to hours.

Amy could only think about a wedding march.

13

THE WEDDING MARCH

Sacramento, CA – 7:30 a.m., October 13th, 2020

Two weeks didn't seem like a long enough time to plan a march, but in the world of wedding planning, two weeks might as well have been an eternity. Or at least, certainly long enough to have transported a cadre to the city of Sacramento and California's state capitol.

Spread around the city were any number of other event planners, photographers, florists, caterers, and more, ready to dress to the nines and march later that morning. But just how many of those had actually made the journey was an intrusive worry that Amy tried not to dwell on.

You learn a lot about human nature in event planning, and human nature can be flaky. Amy could plan a wedding perfectly, yet the one thing she didn't control was confirming which guests would attend on the big day. On the other hand, people try to crash weddings because they're fun, free, and sometimes even societally advantageous, and a protest didn't have that same draw. Today, there wouldn't be free food, a social ladder, or even fold-out chairs. There were any number of reasons that the tens and hundreds of invitees might choose to drop out.

Amy tried not to think about these things as she walked the planned path of the march, which would begin a few hours later.

The state's capitol mall sat with an eerie quiet in the early morning hours of Tuesday, October 13th. The occasional street sweeper made its way down the road, pausing to circle around a Prius with condensation on its windows, which would undoubtedly be sporting a parking ticket when Amy would return with her sign and wedding gown.

It wasn't clear whether she should feel awed or intimidated by the towering capitol rotunda, which stood atop the colonnade of four sequoia-sized columns. Today, Amy would feel elements of both, but hoped it would be more of the former than the latter. She especially hoped she would be awed by the power of democracy and the right to assemble, rather than the futility of taking a gamble.

In the shadow of the building, Amy struggled to remember the last time she'd prayed this much. She had plenty of clients and friends who were firm believers in the motto "let go and let God," but Amy had never let go of anything in her life. When Amy prayed, she prayed that God would look out for that which was out of her control, and to give her the awareness to catch the rest.

Rallying more than twenty or thirty protesters that morning—giving these struggling business owners, colleagues, and friends the gall to participate—was not something any human being could conjure. The luck of finding success, if those folks did assemble, was even more elusive.

Amy studied the layout of the capitol mall, ensuring that someone inside that stone citadel would hear their commotion. And if they were lucky, that would be someone with the power to do something.

"Good morninggg," Amy said into her selfie camera, the steps behind her, broadcasting to her personal Instagram account in a pink jacket, pink aviators, and a sequined mask lowered to her chin.

What came next wasn't anything out of the ordinary, just one final message to the troops that one of their many leaders was ready to carry the banner.

It was the same thing she'd written a week earlier to the Facebook group, which had only grown in its fervor during this time. CAPE, the San Diego Event Coalition, and so many other groups and users had managed to increase the temperature around demanding recognition in the eyes of their government.

"Join CAPE in Sacramento on Oct 13th…. CAPE is advocating for the SAFE reopening of private events using the already approved state guidelines for Places of Worship and Restaurants. Events are not even listed as an industry, and we need you to get our message through to our State Leaders. It's time we get off the sidelines and use our voices."

The pieces had come together remarkably fast, and with no small thanks to a local venue owner. Suffering from empty venues across the state, the venue owner took no hesitation partnering with CAPE to take a stand.

The protest later that morning would begin at the Sterling Hotel, which sat conveniently only a half mile from the state capitol, as Amy had presently confirmed.

Once the board knew the venue owner was on board, planning the march became a call to action. Looking at Amy in her video, you'd never know just how truly nervous she was about that call. Only a few more last-second cancellation texts like she'd already received, and it would be a pitiful showing. It could be the end of First Comes Love along with it.

The headlines would write themselves. Instead of the excellent search engine optimization Amy had fostered over the past decade, potential clients would just find "Wedding Planner Should Stick to Weddings" written in the *Bee* or the *Union-Tribune* when they searched for her.

After a brisk walk back to the Sacramento Sheraton, midway between the Sterling Hotel and the governor's office, Amy and her family made their way to the back in street clothes. At the hotel, the owner was waiting for them. The Ulkutekins were one of the first arrivals, but like a general on the field of battle, it was crucial that Amy was one of the first in uniform.

"Amy! Hi!"

He greeted her with a quick hug. They both tried to hold their breath for COVID's sake, despite being masked and outdoors.

"Thank you so much for your help. My husband I think you've met. And the kids."

Amy's accompanying trio shook hands politely.

"Well let's do this. Dressing rooms are going to be inside and on your right. We're going to use the back side of the building for the staging. More sidewalk space out there for interviews, if press members stop by."

Moments later, Amy was in her dressing room, staring at the dress she'd brought for the march. The Ulkutekins had made a road trip from San Diego, and this dress was part of that journey. With how tight finances had grown, it just made sense to bring the family in the SUV, rather than buy four roundtrips.

Not to mention, E.J. had been having issues with focus during his learning lately. His meals were beginning to drift further apart or closer together. Amy was trying to keep her attention on him as best she could while she juggled everything else, and that meant loading up into the RAV4 and playing "I Spy" across the Golden State.

The family had made their first stop in Orange County at a dress shop to pick up a dress, tuxedo, and the kids' ring bearer suit and flower girl dress, in addition to a handful of other gowns for other march attendees and board members.

The shop was nice enough to rent them the dresses for next to nothing, just happy to be a part of the cause. Their vast collection of excellent quality clothing, which they'd made available at low-cost rental rates, was a few more missed rent payments from being totally lost.

"We're so excited to help out. This is huge for us. For all of us," the shop owner had told Amy when she'd walked inside a day before.

After Orange County, it was a couple more hours up the Five until they were able to stop for apple picking in gorgeous San Luis Obispo. This was COVID, so the typical West Coast traffic was taking a much-needed break, allowing for more rapid and eco-friendly transit south-to-north.

At no fault of the dress shop, the gown was a loose fit, which Amy had just now realized. She couldn't complain, since "free" was as good as it gets, but it would still mean her march might be a tad slower than expected. Since she was slated to be one of the upfront folks, it might even work in her favor. She might as well have been one of her many grooms from years past, carefully advised to take their time as they walked down the aisle.

Making her way back to the street, Amy looked around the hotel. Like an East Coast summer resort town in the first week of October, the Sterling was ghostly and vacant. But that was the secret of most venues: they were vacant on most weekdays. On the streets outside, not ones or tens, but hundreds had now gathered.

Masked, socially distanced, and rule-abiding event professionals lined H Street for an entire city block.

Amy felt a weight lifted off her shoulders as they shared grins and chuckles. It was good to see so many of these people again. Getting friends together was the core of event planning, especially weddings, and Amy didn't know how badly she'd missed that until now. She might have just stayed outside reconnecting, were it not for news crews gathering just up the sidewalk.

Within moments of emerging from the Sterling, a reporting team from the *Sacramento Bee* had already waved Amy toward them.

"Tell us about this event," the reporter asked, after laboriously confirming the spelling of Amy's name.

Amy recited the pitch she now knew by heart.

"So we're out here to do a walk for weddings, which is essentially a march to the state capitol, to show them that the event industry has been forgotten. We are one of the very few industries that isn't even listed as a dropdown on the industry list for the state of California. Dog walkers are listed, there's a number of different industries, and all have guidance in the four tiers, but events don't. We need to let the state legislature know…please recognize us."

Looking around, Amy finally felt the group would be difficult to ignore.

They had also done extensive work to deck out the protestors with matching masks in bright orange and purple, which read SAVE PRIVATE EVENTS and WEDDINGS ARE ESSENTIAL.

"We have a number of different people out here today. We have venue operators, planners, florists, deejays. We have some brides and grooms whose weddings have been affected by COVID. We have a cross-section of the industry."

And the cross-section was actively engaging with anyone who chose to listen. CAPE's Facebook Live vlogger walked around to capture in-the-moment interviews while the wedding photographers in the group captured memories right and left.

A tuxedo store owner with slicked back hair, wearing his own sequined suit, reiterated the need for guidance to prevent the unsanctioned events that had run rampant across the state. A musician wearing a gray vest with checkered treble clefs worried about losing his home. A deejay in a pink plaid button-down complained that deejaying for an audience of one, himself, didn't have the same allure, and he wanted to get back to work.

Amy concluded, "We're not asking for a dance party for two hundred people. We understand that's not safe. But really what we need is a seat at the table, and to show people that events can happen safely, and we have guidelines. Use our knowledge. Give us a seat at the table so we can show you how events can happen."

After a few other thoughts and notes that wouldn't make the final cut, the first interview of the day was over. Amy turned back to take in the group that had gathered, trying to enjoy the last still moment.

"Are you local, or San Diego?" the *Bee* reporter asked.

"I'm San Diego," she answered, quickly realizing how presumptive that had sounded, not meaning to take ownership over the city or these activists.

Looking over her shoulder, Amy really wanted to say, "They are San Diego."

They're San Diego, Los Angeles, San Francisco, San Bernardino, Sacramento, Riverside, Palm Springs, and five other California counties, if not more.

It was a few more minutes before the final attendees had gathered, most of them able to take cover in the shade of the hotel and the tree-lined sidewalks. When the group had circled around, and after Amy had garnered a round of applause for their host, she announced, "We have a few chants, but we'll start with 'save weddings now,' and when we get to the capitol steps, make sure the best dresses and tuxedos get a spot up front. Cool?"

The group cheered, their excitement growing as their numbers surpassed two or three hundred. Amy smiled, ready to hand the proverbial mic over to the group.

"Ready to roll?"

With a louder cheer, the mobilization began, and the chant, "Save weddings now!" grew to a chorus.

As the protest reached the street corner, sirens began to wail. Luckily, they immediately decreased in volume, rather than speeding directly toward them and beginning an arrest.

The march soon stretched over three blocks, winding its way the entire half mile from the Sterling to the steps of the state capitol building. There weren't too many eyes on the group in its first block, as it passed parking garages and closed offices.

But by the time they'd passed a few J Street fast food joints, and turned toward the California State Capitol Park, people began to pay attention, pulling out smartphones and cameras to share the bizarre sight. Passing vehicles honked in support too, except for a police SUV, which bisected the throng.

"That was a ranger, don't worry!" CAPE's vlogger called to the back half of the march, as the SUV disappeared down the street, the crosswalk's ADA accessible chirping alerting them it was time to rejoin the group.

The protest made its way across the final crossing into the capitol park, beneath the six block-long row of palm trees, stretching from the Plaza de California all the way to the rose garden. They passed the state treasurer's office and the third district appellate courthouse before turning East for the final half block march up to the capitol steps.

"What are we trying to save?!" the organizers asked those in tow.

"Save weddings now!" the crowd replied, more fervently than ever, as they spread out to take their places, turning to face the Capitol Mall with the building to their backs.

The vlogger chuckled, still holding the phone up, watching a phalanx of wedding planners taking charge and doing what they do best: arranging wedding party members for photos.

"This is what happens when you get wedding planners and coordinators putting on a protest!"

Amy looked to her right and left at the crowd, which began to properly arrange itself on two sets of four steps, separated by one slightly larger step.

"How does it look? I like it," the venue owner asked, as he sorted the final brides upfront. Amy turned toward the group and nodded. This was beyond what she'd envisioned, and it was thrilling.

The Facebook live video asked her to say a few words before joining the group.

"We are here! We are fighting," she said, holding her own poster, which in spite of her own above average height, was half as tall as she was.

It read, "WEDDINGS CAN BE DONE SAFELY - LET US WORK!"

Fellow board member Sean began the chant, walking back and forth in front of the protestors, throwing his hands in the air.

"What do we need?" he shouted from behind his mask.

"Guidelines!" the group chanted.

"Save weddings!"

"Now!" they answered.

He and Amy turned to face the media, now one with the protest.

"Save weddings now!"

"Save weddings now!"

"SAVE WEDDINGS NOW!"

The chant reached a fever pitch and continued for another ten minutes.

In true event planner fashion, the wireless microphone and speaker setup was ready to go, as Sean welcomed Amy to the center of the makeshift marble stage.

Finally standing on the steps of the state capitol, and with a voice loud enough that no one inside could ignore it, Amy adjusted her veil and mask, which were continuing to limit her range of motion.

The second major win for the protest was the gathering of members of the media and general public, who were witnesses to the protest. Without the public's approval, their protest was meaningless. And the nodding, the cheers, and the social media attention emboldened them. It had all come together magically, and now it was time to bring it home.

Somewhere in the building behind Amy sat Newsom, CDPH, or someone, anyone, who they'd tried to reach these past months. Today, they were listening, because they finally had no choice.

"Perfect!" she began, with more meanings than one.

"How is it that weddings are illegal? This is insane!... We need Governor Newsom and the California Legislature to please help us!... We just want to get back to work."

Amy turned to her right, where the San Francisco planners stood, grinning under their masks.

"We have twelve counties represented here, from San Diego to Sonoma!"

The rest of Amy's speech wasn't much different than the morning news interview, but it still felt good to say it all again, even the bit about dog walkers having more recognition than an industry of millions.

Sean took the mic next.

"I have had to worry not only about my husband and my two kids, but my entire company that I will not let see fail. This state won't fail us. We won't allow it!... We will get open! We will have guidelines! We will be heard!"

He took a deep breath and continued, "I can stand in a Costco line with two hundred and fifty people in a warehouse, but I can't sit with family and friends at a dinner table!"

The crowd knowingly laughed.

"I don't care. Straight, gay, whatever you want to be. Love is love!"

After more applause, and speeches by other business owners, a young couple stepped up. The groom's hair was slicked to the side and the bride was blonde, wearing a pointed gown.

"How's this for a little bit of irony? Not only am I an event industry member. But I'm a groom."

He waved to his fiancée, who struggled up the stairs to his side.

"We were scheduled to get married this past September.... Not only were we out of work these past seven months, but we also weren't able to celebrate the most meaningful day of our life.... I just felt alone. I just felt afraid. What was going to happen? How was the future going to turn out for us? But I'm so happy to see all of us coming together to fight in the name of love."

He pointed toward the upper windows of the building.

"Governor Newsom, hear us out! We just want to get married! When do we want to get married?!"

"Now!" the crowd cheered, again.

After a couple more speeches, there was one final speaker—rather, a pair of speakers—who were ready for their moment in the spotlight.

"Ariana and E.J. have a couple of words," Sean announced, as he waved them to the steps of the capitol. Amy brimmed with pride as they leapt and bounded step-by-step to Sean's side, leaning into the microphone as Sean bent down to their level.

"These are our youngest members of CAPE," Sean joked.

"What do you guys have to say?"

In unison, the six- and seven-year-old chanted, "Get our mom back to work! Get our mom back to work! Get our mom back to work!" to laughs and more applause.

While the chant had been Amy's idea, she knew that the kids were ready for her to be able to focus on productive work again. It was getting back to work that would stop her from having to play catch-up and activist day-in and day-out. She would finally have nights and weekends with them again.

Not to mention, they wanted good Christmas presents in a few more weeks, and activism didn't pay nearly as well as event planning.

The cheers, the chants, and the protest wrapped up an hour after they'd arrived at the capitol building. And CAPE, SDEC, and the others collectively felt good, not knowing if they'd made a difference or not.

While the protest's attention was focused on the stone bricks that rose stories behind, it was the lawn just to the side of the building where their words also landed on receptive ears. A board member ran up to Amy as they began their walk back toward the Sterling, narrowly escaping the rising sun of an unseasonably warm Sacramento day.

"Amy!"

She looked excited.

"They were outside… they'd, they'd just come back from lunch."

"Who?" Amy asked.

"Two of Newsom's advisors."

Amy couldn't help but smile.

That was about as great a birthday present as she could have hoped for.

***

Somewhere on the Five – October 15th, 2020

From the passenger seat, Amy typed madly as the RAV4 made its way back toward San Diego.

"On Tuesday we marched to the state capitol building to demand guidelines for events. The rally had nearly 200 event professionals from all across California. We had media from every major network and coverage was picked up by AP, so it has gone nationwide. Newsom's Cabinet Secretary Ana Matosantos and Special Advisor to the Governor Angie Wei both were outside and listening to our speeches. It literally could not have gone better.

Yesterday, I met in person with Dr. Alice Chen and her team at California Health and Human Services. They are the ones who draft the industry guidelines. I explained the issues our industry is facing. They said that based on my communication with them, they are actively working on guidelines for private events. She asked me to send over guidance from other states who have done it well, so we are pulling that to send. She is going to tap us for guidance as they work on private event guidelines, so that is promising. Also, Alice included Dr. Pan on our email chain, which is also promising. She said that they will work with GO-Biz on everything; however, I have our lobbyist working on setting up a meeting with GO-Biz directly as I want to make sure things are progressing as quickly as possible.

Since Newsom's cabinet secretary Ana Matosantos and special advisor to the governor Angie Wei both were outside and listening to our speeches, I decided to shoot them an email yesterday to see if we could set up a follow-up meeting, completely not expecting a response. Ana actually wrote me back and agreed to setting up a meeting. Her assistant is cross-referencing schedules, and we are hoping to meet by early next week. Apparently, we created quite the buzz in Sacramento and are a topic of conversation at the capitol.

A HUGE thank you to my fellow CAPE board members for everything you did and continue to do for the reopening efforts. If you haven't already, please join CAPE. We really need additional financial resources to continue working with the legislature. Please know that every cent goes directly to these efforts. Myself and the other board members personally paid for all of our travel and expenses for the rally. We'll continue to keep you posted."

There wasn't much else to say than that. It would be a new day in San Diego as Amy sent the post.

"AMY FOR PRESIDENT" rose to the top of the comment feed.

She couldn't reject that idea quickly enough.

14
INFIDELITY

Sacramento, CA – November 16th, 2020

"One thing you never get used to as a politician is seeing yourself burned in effigy."

Gavin had written those words in Citizenville almost a decade ago. This evening, the national headlines gave him that same pit in his stomach. Were it not for the increasingly cold Northern California Fall turning to Winter, there very well might have been effigies of Gavin around the state tonight.

He understood the rage. He had made a mistake, and at the worst possible inflection point in this year of pandemic.

It was now less than 24 hours since a video went viral, which showed the governor dining at the French Laundry restaurant. He dined with a group of friends that was larger than guidelines for certain parts of the state.

I'm not perfect.

Of all the things that politicians got a bad rap for, "rules for thee, but not for me" was one saying that Gavin desperately wished never to succumb to. Gavin deeply respected the rules and progress made since the start of the pandemic in California. They'd undoubtedly saved lives and led the nation in a time of crisis.

He bristled any time he thought about what folks at the highest levels of government would whisper amongst themselves.

"The public is incapable of understanding the nuances of this, so let's not tell them the whole truth," they'd nod along with each other.

Yet, Gavin had already proven this wrong with how forthcoming the state had been with its COVID metrics. In all other areas, Gavin thought this yearning for privacy was wrong for public figures, even when that video of him had popped up on the news.

It was Wim Elfrink who had taught him, "It used to be 'Big Brother is watching you.'… Now, it's 'We, the citizens, are watching you.'" And he'd thought it good, because it gave his citizens more power.

Whereas other scandals and nothingburgers had been spurred by right-wing media, this criticism couldn't be dismissed as partisan. The people of Gavin's idyllic Citizenville were too unhappy with him to just take a "no comment" approach.

Tonight, it was time to face the music, yet it was at a poor moment for such a misstep. Cases in California had doubled in the past ten days. The situation was suddenly dire again after months of easing case numbers.

For that video to have burst onto the stage at this moment could lead to dire consequences for those who were considering bucking the rules for the Thanksgiving holiday, now only a week away. So the governor's update didn't begin with a measured walk to the podium. This was about being direct, even if it felt like slow-motion to him.

This was about saving lives at a time when the media broadcast the opposite.

"Just addressing some of the national headlines…. Daily cases, though, in the state of California have doubled just in the last ten days. This is simply the fastest increase California has seen since the beginning of this pandemic."

While the governor's Facebook streams had been growing steadily in viewership in the earliest days of the pandemic, those numbers had since slowed. Tonight, the stream would be back near that quarter million mark.

As usual, Gavin chose to put himself last. Perhaps a half hour was too long to put off discussion of his apology, but he thought it wise. With all the eyes returning, they might be made explicitly aware of the danger of COVID's newest wave, rather than his explanation.

The data that he so admired appeared on screen in between his video cell and the one belonging to the ASL interpreter. The chart showed an increase in cases over 50%, which topped even June's rapid rise in case counts, which for the period of June 15th to 21st, the chart put at under 40%.

Today wasn't about leading off with an apology. It was about tightening control. The measures put in place hadn't staved off the case increase, so the administration had opted to double down.

"Some counties will move multiple tiers, not just for example, yellow to orange or orange to red…. Counties that move back also must make industry or sectoral changes urgently."

A bearish map reminiscent of July's tier announcement appeared now, but this one made its predecessor look like a walk in the park.

"40 counties now will be moving backwards in the state. You'll see and I'll show you again in the original last week's tiered status. 13 counties in purple, 22 in red. Today we have 41 counties in purple, 11 in red, less in orange."

The next part flew a little too close to the sun, and Gavin realized it may have been worth addressing the French Laundry before his frequent guest speaker, Health Secretary Ghaly Took, the podium.

Dr. Ghaly opened, "We know when people gather with people they don't live with, often our close friends, even family members, we think that it's OK to put your guard down."

Gavin was happy not to be on camera for one of the first times in his life. His face wasn't reddening, but there wasn't a good facial expression to make when facing a comment like that.

"We think it's OK to take off your mask even for a little bit, to enjoy a drink or enjoy a meal. But it's exactly those moments that might create a high transmission risk. So we urge you to consider how you engage with friends and family over the weeks to come to keep transmission rates low," Ghaly continued.

After a few more sets of data, the governor was able to retake the podium and concluded the written portion of the broadcast.

"Wash your hands and minimize mixing."

"Now, on the 'minimize mixing,' I would be remiss if I did not acknowledge something, just before we go into the Q&A."

A sheepish grin crept onto the Governor's face as he retook the podium.

"I very soberly acknowledge that a few weeks ago, I was asked to join a friend's fiftieth birthday."

Accompanied by a few gesticulations and hand waves, Gavin leapt into his apology, but not before a fleeting excuse.

"A friend that I've known for almost twenty years had…put a lot of time and energy into his fiftieth birthday."

Luckily, the governor explained, this party took place in Napa, "Which was in the orange status, relatively loose compared to some other counties."

He added the restaurant was outdoors too, for good measure.

"As soon as I sat down at the larger table, I realized it was a little larger group than I had anticipated. And I made a bad mistake. Instead of sitting down," he paused for a moment, changing his tone slightly, "I should have 'stood up,' and walked back to my car, and driven back to my house."

The "standing up" line was supposed to have a double meaning, but that worked better on paper than it did in reality. He tried to audible out of it and did so almost seamlessly.

"You can quibble about the guidelines et cetera, et cetera, but the spirit of what I'm preaching all the time was contradicted. And I gotta own that. So I want to apologize to you, because I need to preach and practice, and not just preach and not practice."

The words were starting to tumble as the apology continued. Gavin's grin was now a full smile, as the weight of the almost-scandal had been lifted.

"We're all human. We all fall short sometimes. We've been out I think, three times—in fact, I know it's been three times because I remember all of those dinners very very vividly. Uh, since February. Just three times, twice with my wife, and once by myself, outdoors, and then this occasion. And there were just a few extra people there than the spirit of what I'm promoting."

The apology and its excuses repeated over the next thirty to forty seconds, almost as if a teleprompter had accidentally rewound and played twice. The governor was smiling, almost chuckling by the time the statement reached its end.

His previously published words echoed in his mind yet again.

Get the information out there before someone else reports it about you, as that's the only way to control it.

It was George Clooney who had told him, "Scandal is huge, but it only lasts for a minute. And then it doesn't stick."

Gavin was certain that would be the case tonight, as he reached the end of the presser.

"COVID fatigue is exhausting and I'm empathetic beyond words. I'm not here to browbeat anybody. I'm here to find the higher angels in the spirit that is this moment to try to work through and get through this sprint, get to those vaccines, where that light really is at the end of the tunnel."

With that, it was over, and he could move on, not that he found questions from members of the press to be wholly relaxing. It was usually the greatest thorn in his side, because it was the one variable he couldn't totally plan for.

With great fortune, his first question from the Associated Press wasn't about the scandal.

Adam Beam asked, "There's no distinction between a business operating responsibly and one that isn't. So what do you tell these businesses that are playing by the rules and are frustrated and angry…. And what is the benefit to them of doing what the state says they must do if they will still be penalized?"

15
THE NON-COVID CASE

San Diego, CA – December 24th, 2020

"The irrepressible Judge Judith Sheindlin continues to hold court as presiding judge on Judge Judy, the highest-rated daily, half-hour, nationally syndicated daytime television program in American history."

Amy had been refreshing JudgeJudy.com every week for the past month and had almost memorized the site's adjective-laden description at this point.

She hoped there would be another week before what she knew was coming, but the site refresh over the weekend had confirmed it, just after the production had updated its weekly schedule of shows. Thursday, December 24th's preview was a twenty-second clip of Amy behind the defendant's stand.

She'd tried not to spend her day thinking about what was imminent from the depths of Emmy Award-winning CBS daytime television. She tried instead to focus on wrapping gifts for E.J. and Ariana. It was Christmas Eve after all. It was just her luck that CBS had given her episode of Judge Judy primetime treatment.

Going on the popular courtroom show was somewhere between a no-brainer and a terrible idea. When Amy had received the letter of request from the producer, it was worded almost exactly the same as a letter she'd received ten years before.

It's very difficult to go far in the world of small business without having to face small claims court, whether that's as a plaintiff or defendant. Luckily, that decade-old case centered around a dog that had attacked Amy during a walk and didn't involve First Comes Love, in its infancy at the time.

That case hadn't made it to Judge Judy, because the plaintiff had dropped out at the last moment. But this time, both Amy and one of her clients, the plaintiff in this case, had chosen to go through with it.

Arriving at the studio, Amy was antsy, but not nervous. The production asked for a COVID test before Amy got to set, in addition to a rapid test once she'd stepped foot on the Sunset Boulevard backlot. And of course, "Absolutely NO WHITE clothing."

If anything, Amy was able to take note of the many precautions that her industry had begged for, which were under full swing for one of California's most critical industries, not to mention at a time when cases were at their highest point on record.

The producers had arranged the ubiquitous Star Wagons as COVID-safe green rooms for each contestant. (And yeah, that "contestant" moniker felt strange but was technically correct.)

Knowing the ins and outs of entertainment, Amy dreaded being coached by one of the producers, one of whom she could already hear in the trailer next door, hyping up another contestant for a different case that would tape that morning, back to back with hers.

The walls were so thin, it had been impossible for Amy to even hear herself think. She didn't regret eavesdropping under those circumstances, and it made her self-done hair and makeup session less stressful.

The producer playfully sparred, "You better buck up! Pay attention. You go argue for yourself. Defend yourself on television, 'kay? You got almost three thousand on the line. That's coming outta your pocket!"

Then they hesitated.

"Well, I mean, it ain't coming outta your pocket. You know that."

"Yeah," a man agreed.

"But people watching don't know that. The second this microphone goes in your pocket, it's that cash money. You got me?"

"Yeah!"

The producer wrapped up with a great line, something Amy wished she could say to her brides and grooms before walking down the aisle.

"I want REAL emotion, REAL thoughts, REAL *shit!*"

Each contestant was oblivious to the fact that their opponents received the same routine to create the most engaging conflict when the cameras went live. This same producer would go to this guy's opponent and tell him or her that they were in fact owed their cash money all the same as he was.

The producer was more than happy to oblige when Amy begged to be left alone. One less routine having to be performed from behind an N-95 was nothing to turn down. She obliged Amy with a smirk and a shrug.

"Hey, you do you. Don't get me fired though, 'kay?"

The producer saw that same look in Amy's eye that Kevin Gordon had: she didn't need anything more than to be told where to hit her mark and whom to address.

"Real emotion, thoughts, and shit," Amy promised with a nod.

The producer closed her door, moving on to the next trailer.

Amy's plaintiffs were a couple she'd planned and then rescheduled. They'd paid her standard deposit and signed on the dotted line. And after Amy had done the work to plan not one wedding, but two, they chose to elope, and wanted the entire deposit refunded.

This was one of the many sticky scenarios that had played out over the past eight or nine months. A deposit was there for a reason and ensured that the immense lead-up work to a wedding wouldn't be ruined by a bounced check, runaway bride, or worse. And COVID had proven to be even worse than a groom left at the altar.

Even the most shortsighted client deserved Amy's most earnest effort. That was what had turned First Comes Love into a behemoth: kindness. Plus, it wasn't her client's job to have foresight. It was hers.

But when this couple came for their entire deposit, especially after Amy had done the work twice, and was willing to do it a third time, she had to put her foot down. Even then, she offered to split the deposit with them, which they'd refused.

Amy knew her case was solid on paper, and from her experience in that unavoidable small claims arena, what was on paper superseded just about everything else. Yet there was still the nagging worry that she'd bitten off more than she could chew by putting it on daytime TV.

For Amy, today wasn't about winning. It was about shining a spotlight on the plight of her industry, and with the help of one of television's most-watched shows. But that came at the risk of First Comes Love, which she fully recognized. If her case fell apart, it would be just as damaging as a lack of protesters on the capitol steps would've been two months before.

On the plus side, the show paid the winnings. For all its good, small claims court is notoriously helpless when it comes to receiving what's owed. You don't have the ability to send a collections agency after a neighbor who backed into your mailbox, but on Judge Judy, you didn't have to. Big Ticket Television most likely reached into the extensive coffers of their parent company, CBS Studios, who then probably billed their parent company Paramount, for the comparably measly amount.

As silly as it all seemed, Amy was thrilled when a production assistant knocked at her trailer door just before 10 a.m. and she could get it over with.

"Amy? We're ready for you."

No one had attempted calling her "Mrs. Ulkutekin" that morning. That saved all of them plenty of time. These television producers knew their limits.

Amy and her assistant-turned-witness made their way into the brisk morning air, across the backlot, and through a stage door with the customary notice, DO NOT ENTER WHEN LIGHT IS BLINKING.

Passing beneath the non-blinking light and onto the soundstage, Amy was reminded of her time before First Comes Love, especially seeing those bright lights, bustling crewmembers, and the smell of whatever catering had begun cooking for lunch. It might as well be the hotel or the airline event all over again.

The usual side table with coffee, snacks, and other drinks looked comical in the age of COVID: individually wrapped apples, granola bars, and even plastic-bagged donuts.

The lack of a courtroom ceiling also didn't faze Amy, nor did the plaintiffs entering from the other side of the stage. If anything, this was going to be the final time having to see or hear from them, and that was welcome after all the toxicity.

What did surprise Amy was who, or what, awaited her as she took her podium: a massive flat screen television.

Judy Sheindlin was working from home too, it seemed.

The TV judge offered the contestants a curt grin, flipping through her notes she'd prepared for the next taping, as the contestants of the case prior made their exit.

It wasn't long at all before the next "camera speed" was called, and the lights and camera prepared for "action." It was some of the fastest and most efficient work Amy had ever seen, which made sense considering this show had accomplished a couple thousand episodes over multiple decades.

But that was all weeks before. The actual taping had gone by so quickly that Amy barely remembered most of the crucial moments, struggling to piece together what she'd said in case she had to defend it to peers or clients.

Continuing to dig presents out of the hiding spots in her house, Amy turned on the bedroom TV and tried not to hyper-fixate on what came next.

"The people are real! The cases are real! The rulings are final! This is Judge Judy."

Amy hadn't watched the show closely enough to catch all the details in the theme song: the riff on Beethoven's Fifth, the winking Lady Justice figure, or the clever design of the title. To be fair, most don't know much about the show, besides what they may have watched while at a delicatessen or in a DMV's waiting room.

The show expertly weaved together the asynchronous production with the real-life Judy, Amy, and the client. You'd never know about the flatscreen TV, and Amy had almost forgotten entirely, watching it back today.

"I hired her as a 'day-of' coordinator, and there never was a 'day' at all. She has my money, and I want it back," opened the plaintiff, saying plenty to that effect.

Amy responded with her practiced retorts: 'day-of' coordination fees covered both the day and the work that led up to the day, despite there being less work than a full contract might have demanded. That was time she'd devoted to her client and away from her family, other clients, and so many others.

Moreover, Amy had incurred actual costs by putting staff on hold for the day, and in turn paying their deposits. When the plaintiff chose not to go forward with their day, those deposits couldn't be taken back any more easily than Amy's could.

When Amy mentioned the coordination that had gone into the couple's wedding, the plaintiff argued they'd never seen or received those details. Judy leaned in when Amy revealed she'd brought the email chain.

"Let me see that," Judy asked.

Amy handed the papers to the bailiff, and the Judge lowered her glasses to read. Judy looked back up, toward the plaintiff.

"I'm looking at your name on these emails. Sure seems like you knew what was going on."

The plaintiff, wishing to move on from this newly uncomfortable position, rolled her eyes and retorted, "Amy was supposed to be my 'day-of' coordinator. The day never happened. I don't see what else there is to it!"

The contract was the final nail in the coffin and put to bed any other issues that the plaintiff brought up. When Amy produced that document, they had entered the endgame.

Tired of hearing "day-of" repeated ad nauseam, Judy looked back and forth between Amy and the other side of the TV courtroom.

"Don't you get it?" she asked the plaintiff, whose pulse began to race as the room went silent.

"She worked hard for you. I don't care what kind of contract you signed with her, or what its name was. She did the work. I've gotten married, my own kids have gotten married, and these planners handle it all. She's done her work, and she fulfilled her contractual obligation. That's the deal."

Judy clacked the gavel, and it was over.

With all due respect to the next case and the commercial breaks in between, Amy shut off the TV and breathed a sigh of relief. In the end, it went about as well as it could have. It was hard to see herself on camera, yet again, but that was the case for just about anyone in her shoes.

Despite the black TV screen, her Judy experience hadn't come to a close. Amy soon learned there were other facets of being a Judy contestant. First, her Facebook messenger app exploded with different messages from potential suitors across the country. These were unexpected, unwelcome, and thankfully, fairly easy to block.

What wasn't as easy to navigate was her ringing phone.

Being a small business owner, getting a call on a weekend or even on Christmas Eve from an unknown number wasn't out of the ordinary.

"Hi, is this Amy?" a woman asked on the other end of the line, a rural drawl somewhat detectable. The number wasn't a familiar one, and Amy wasn't expecting a client call.

"Yes," Amy replied, trying to keep a roll of tape from sticking to her fingers.

"I just saw you on TV, and I gotta say, you are the most–"

That was as far as it needed to go. Amy hung up before the first adjective could reach her ear, which luckily had been lost forever, somewhere between flyover country and a Chula Vista cell tower.

The caller left a grating voicemail another minute later.

"Hi, you just hung up on me," she'd started, as if that wasn't immediately clear.

It wasn't like Amy had other anonymous callers that cussed or sounded this much like Kathy Bates.

"I just wanna let you know, I just saw the episode of Judge Judy, and you should be fuckin' ashamed of your fat ass for takin' people's money durin' this time so your fat ass can get some free money. You should be ashamed, and I'm sure other people are gonna be pissed off too. Hope your business goes to shit!"

Amy wondered if, a few hours later, the same woman might be standing in a church pew singing "Silent Night."

Merry Christmas to you too, ma'am. And a happy new year.

Amy considered deleting the voicemail along with her suitors' continuing attempts to woo her. For posterity's sake, she didn't.

The presents were finally finished, and Amy could return to the living room with the rest of the family. That night, they'd have a Christmas dinner that was the best Amy could do on their dwindling budget.

Across the country, still occupied with the second segment of the Judy episode, COVID cases were surging, far beyond what anyone had feared earlier in the pandemic.

While the new strain of the disease had proven to trade increased contagiousness for a decreased lethality, both had accelerated beyond any previous measure. Every tier in California was dark purple, and for the first time, cases had accelerated so much that it wasn't even worth thinking about asking for future guidance.

The only upcoming event for CAPE was on January 6th, which they'd dubbed "Save Events Day," featuring personal stories from their fellow out-of-work industry members.

If anything, they'd hoped the event might lead to additional financial support. The businesses closed for this third wave had been shuttered for a month, whereas the events industry was about to embark on their tenth.

Even CAPE's efforts to draw attention to the January 6th social media campaign would fall short though, because that January 6th would prove to be the January 6th.

That was just the tip of the iceberg though.

If 2020 was some kind of purgatory for Amy, stuck between agency and helplessness, 2021 would begin with utter Hell.

16
BREAKING POINT

San Diego, CA – January 20th, 2021

Amy was surprised the lollipop bowl was still in the pediatrician's waiting room. She and E.J. both had to go through a temperature check and remain masked throughout the check-in process. They'd been socially distanced too before they were escorted to room four.

Finally able to lick the candy, E.J. tried to gulp down as much of the sucker as he could before another doctor or nurse practitioner stepped into their room. Amy reached out and brushed his knee.

"It's gonna be OK."

He nodded.

It had been a rough week for Amy's son, so if the fruit-flavored pop eased that, she'd make sure he'd get that at the very least.

Amy had thought E.J. was suffering from COVID at first, but they wouldn't get the chance for those test results to come back. Amy didn't even have time to write down the testing appointment details by the time she'd gotten the call from the school that morning.

E.J. had experienced an upset stomach, meaning his lethargy was less likely to be COVID, and more likely to be something else entirely. Unfortunately, they had no idea what that might be. If the doctor didn't have any ideas, it would mean more virtual schooling and less time spent on tracking vaccine rollout, which Amy had eagerly watched and waited for.

San Diego, and nearly every other county in the state, was still squarely in the purple tier, still suffering the compounded hangover of the holiday season, which would be the world's last without a COVID vaccine. But that wouldn't last if those vaccines were the real deal. When the herd immunity numbers were reached, it very well could be over and done with.

At least, that was Amy's current understanding.

A knock at the door came more quickly than Amy was used to, especially at this office, which was usually swamped with other parents like her, caring for kids who'd also been excused from school.

"We all ready?" the pediatrician asked.

E.J. mustered a smile and didn't even think to reaffix his mask, nor was he asked to.

"Thanks for fitting us in on short notice," Amy said.

"We're pretty busy around here, but never too busy for my trooper, E.J."

E.J. smiled a little bigger. Amy reached out to touch his knee, trying to communicate as much care as she could from behind her mask.

"Been feeling queasy lately, buddy?"

E.J. nodded.

"I threw up," he boasted, as any boy his age would.

The doctor nodded.

"We don't want that to happen again, huh?"

E.J. shook his head as the doctor unfurled the instruments usually administered by one of the nurses.

Amy didn't think twice about it at the time, but gradually, she began to realize this visit wasn't like any before.

"Can you say, 'ahh' for me?"

E.J. parted his purple lips.

"Ahhh."

The doctor turned to Amy.

"His lips were a normal color before coming in, right?"

Amy grinned and nodded.

"Assumed that was the case. Always good to ask."

Next came the stethoscope, thermometer, and all that other stuff.

Amy distracted her mind with the small details of the room, and the even smaller text on each item: oseltamivir phosphate, sphygmomanometer, albuterol sulfate, and the rest. It was all she knew to do in the moment, having been through this routine so many times before.

As the pediatrician began typing on a tablet, Amy realized he may not have realized the nurse had taken these measurements when they first came in. She could at least save him a few minutes.

"I think they checked his blood pressure when we came in, if that helps."

The doctor nodded, more intensely focused than Amy had realized.

"Yes, I see that here. Thank you. Just wanted to double-check. Or see if it had changed."

"Oh, of course," Amy apologized, not realizing that a finger-mounted device was in fact different from what they'd used on E.J. a few minutes earlier.

"That one gets the pulse too, right?"

"I'm looking at blood oxygen."

"Oh."

This was usually where the doctor would shake his head and say something placating like "nothing to worry about."

After a short pause, no such phrase followed.

The silence grew deafening as E.J. twiddled his clean lollipop stick in his fingers.

"I'll be right back. Just another moment."

Once that moment had passed, only seconds in real life, but hours in Amy's head, he returned with another nurse.

"So E.J., we're going to go for a little ride. Would that be cool with you?"

E.J. nodded and smiled more weakly than ever, as the doctor produced another lollipop for him, alongside a paper cup of water.

Turning to Amy, and still with a voice projecting indelible calm, the doctor explained, "We've called the ambulance, and we're going to get you over to Rady's."

Amy wondered if there was some mistake. Maybe they were in the wrong room.

"What's wrong?"

Her mask muffled anything else.

"We don't think it's worth taking chances on right now. It looks a lot like D.K.A."

Sensing Amy's sudden panic, the pediatrician posed a follow-up question.

"Do you or your husband have a family history of diabetes?"

***

San Diego, CA – January 26th, 2021

"Here comes the prick. Hold on tight to Boo Bear."

E.J. obeyed, grabbing the stuffed bear that the EMTs had given him on their ride to Rady's Children Hospital, now almost a week ago. It was a long stay, one which they'd just returned from.

This was their second or third finger prick since getting home, and thanks to Boo Bear, they'd get through this one without incident, and the others to follow.

The most important thing, despite all they'd suffered since the previous Wednesday, was that E.J. was alive. Not until Amy had been able to catch her breath at her son's hospital bedside and started Googling the many acronyms spread across his chart, did she realize what a close call it had all been.

Amy would quickly learn that D.K.A., or diabetic ketoacidosis, was a symptom of type 1 diabetes, the type that isn't caused by a bad diet or lack of exercise later in life. In essence, his organs had begun to shut down due to increased acids in his blood, which all stemmed from issues with his pancreas, and so on.

The medical definitions had come earlier in the week, before the nutritionists, psychologists, and every other facet of "caring for a diabetic family member 101" began. The more recent details, which would keep E.J. healthy, were what Amy remembered better than the initial human biology lesson.

They told her that D.K.A. was the symptom that informed something like a fifth of type 1 diabetics that they had the condition at all. So Amy wasn't at fault for not realizing it. It wasn't anyone's fault.

Most importantly, E.J. would make a full recovery. And thank God for that. (Amy certainly did.)

At the moment, she hadn't thought about the aftermath, because she was focused on the short-term. Once the pace of the medical treatment had slowed and it was obvious that the Ulkutekins had avoided tragedy, those secondary thoughts bubbled to the surface.

What would E.J.'s care look like? Did the family have the resources to care for E.J., or would one parent have to swap work hours for responsibilities like testing and specialized meals? How much more time and effort would meals require, now that E.J.'s blood sugar was so delicate?

And then, inevitably, came the questions of cost.

When it comes to health, you don't want to start griping about money. Money doesn't matter when someone's life hangs in the balance.

But Amy couldn't avoid the question any longer as E.J.'s finger prick came back healthy, and he returned to virtual school at the edge of her desk, beginning to act like his old self again.

She reluctantly checked the prices of smartphones on her office computer. While she never saw herself as the kind of person to put a smartphone in the hands of a seven-year-old, it was unavoidable now that they'd decided on getting him a glucose monitor.

The glucose monitor was just the latest addition to their diabetic shopping cart. The test strips, finger prick kits, syringes, healthy foods, and three different types of insulin added up fast, and wouldn't abate anytime soon. Nor would the weekly checkup visits to the doctor or diabetic clinic, and costs associated with those. And that was on top of the five days and nights at Rady's, complete with doctors, nurses, nutritionists, psychologists, social workers, and maybe a clown or Elvis impersonator, who'd all seemed to stick their heads in the door at some point that week, and billed for their time afterward. (Except for Elvis, of course, who was a generous volunteer.)

She cross-referenced the smartphone site with her service provider's, seeking some kind of discount or payment plan that would fit within their finances, which were officially reaching zero, and had been even before the medical bills had started to compound.

"Yeah, it was scary, but it was also kinda weird... No, I didn't get French fries until the last day."

E.J. got to do his own little show-and-tell with his classmates, which had lifted his spirits, everyone wanting to sign the proverbial cast on his arm.

Amy smiled and turned back to the site, which had fully loaded, but without the savings she had hoped for.

"Add this many lines and save this little money!"

No dice.

When it came to finances, Amy had always been somewhere between middle class comfort and having the confidence to splurge on her dream Tesla. Her credit card had always been paid off monthly, and she never missed mortgage or car payments. She even maintained those hefty payments as the pandemic raged, far too cautious to miss one in spite of the temporary allowances to do so.

And for the first time, that wouldn't be the case.

Amy opened her bank account and scrolled down past the dwindling checking account balances. She located the credit card section, and with another click, navigated over to the card that still had some breathing room on it, but still less than she'd thought, thanks to another pesky subscription she'd forgotten about.

E.J. waved into his camera as the class wrapped up, and lunchtime was underway. The kids at school would go outside masked, while he would stand alone in his backyard with a sandwich.

"Hey kiddo, can you give me just a sec? I'm about to have a call."

E.J. nodded and hopped out of his seat, hesitating at the door.

"Want me to close your door?"

She'd trained him well. If First Comes Love survived and her son followed in her career footsteps, E.J. might join their co-working space.

"That would be great, honey. Thank you."

As the door closed and Amy turned back to the computer, she finished the phone purchase, maxing out her last credit card, and closed the browser.

She'd partially lied to E.J. There wasn't a meeting. But Amy did need a moment to be alone.

Watching the final pixels of her available credit balance fade away, looking at the still unopened first bill from the hospital, and trying not to dwell on the unfathomable loose ends that had only unraveled further and further since the new year, everything came to a grinding halt.

Emotion took control, and Amy was too exhausted to hold it back this time.

For the first time in over ten months, Amy didn't sob or yell. She got angry.

The feelings of frustration, impatience, and yes, even the other stages of grief Amy had previously denied herself, like sorrow, all took turns within her soul this year. But all the while, she knew that anger was the one thing that never worked like anyone wanted it to.

Anger was the opposite of the scripture she'd heard at so many weddings: "Love is patient, love is kind. It is not jealous, it is not rude, it does not seek its own interests, it is not quick-tempered."

She had acted with love until now, which had kept the quick-tempered feelings at bay. Her love for her career defused her anger at losing it. Her love for her clients held back her temper when others acted impatiently. And her love for her fellow industry members had kept her calm in dealings with each tier of government, no matter how dishonest or dense they might have seemed.

In the spirit of her own business moniker, love had truly come first, and second, and third, and at every stage thereafter.

But what came after love? What came when love hadn't worked?

There were tens of thousands in this state just like Amy, whose jobs were illegal, and had been now for nearly a year. They hadn't received any special stimulus, nor did they have any more of a plan than they had when diseased cruise ships first steamed into Oakland and Los Angeles harbors.

Amy typed three familiar contacts into the TO bar of her email, which were spread across the governor's office and CDPH.

"I am reaching out once again to seek guidelines and inclusion in the state's reopening efforts. It is beyond unacceptable that I have not received a response to the several emails I have sent on behalf of the event industry. We are an entire industry that you have completely ignored and our lives are on the line."

Once calculated in how she'd composed emails, Amy let loose. This would be the fastest email she'd ever write, without all the care about stepping on toes or making enemies.

She didn't care at this point, except about typos. Those were still properly proofread.

"This past week my son went into diabetic ketoacidosis, and we found out he has Type 1 Diabetes. This resulted in a doctor visit, ambulance ride, a hospital stay, and now a lifetime of medication he needs to live. While my business was open, this certainly would have been an adjustment, but now that my business is closed, it is a devastating financial blow.

I've been communicating with you as I burned through my savings. But at least I had savings. At this point, we've been closed nearly an entire year, my savings are gone.... Getting guidelines and being on the reopening plan is no longer a request, it is a necessity for the survival of my family.

Let us operate under the restaurant guidelines. That's all the county needs from you. A few simple words to stop the bleeding. I need to hear back from you immediately and will make myself available at ANY TIME to meet with you."

Amy's pulse raced as adrenaline surged from head to toe.

She hit "send" without much further thought.

Now if it all went to shit, and they all ended up living under a bridge, she'd have truly done everything she could.

***

Nine Hours Later

The red and blue lights flashed as Amy's night vision struggled to adjust.

She was able to count eight officers and three squad cars. The female officer looked at her intently.

"I'm not suicidal. What's going on?"

"The governor's office was concerned after an email they received from you."

Amy grew quiet, feeling like she could have actually said something worrisome in the email. Those emotions of shame were quickly overridden by a sense of ridiculousness as her mental fog cleared.

"I was concerned that they weren't meeting with me. I can't do my job right now."

The officers nodded, seeming like they didn't totally know why they were in Amy's front yard either, especially considering that if Amy had truly been motivated to harm herself, their nine-hour response time wasn't going to do her any favors.

She hadn't swung open the front door wielding a sharp object either, which helped her case.

"So you're doing alright then?" the male officer asked.

"Yeah. Just wanted a meeting."

The female officer reached into her front pocket.

"Well, this is our contact information, if anything changes."

Amy took the card from the officer without looking at it.

"Thanks. You guys can turn the lights off. I mean, we're done here, right?"

The brightness of the lights on all sides had begun to give her a headache.

She was also more than a little self-conscious about what the neighbors were thinking, peering through their blinds.

"Sure. Have a nice night."

The officers turned back to the squad cars. Then their lights turned off, car by car, and the street was soon empty again.

Amy watched the squad peel away and couldn't help but chuckle to herself, whether that was the nervousness dissipating wasn't something she totally could determine one way or another.

Devoting like, eight cops and three cars to her? They probably came all the way from downtown too. Why use such limited resources like that?

Her email hadn't been bad. And even if it was, none of it added up.

Amy made her way inside after one more look down the street.

E.J. and Ariana glanced at her as she closed the door behind her.

"What did the police say?" E.J. asked.

While a white lie about road work or a cat stuck in a tree might have sufficed, Amy had fibbed enough to her son this week.

"They wanted to make sure Mom was OK."

"Are you?" E.J. asked with remarkable maturity.

Amy forced a smile and walked toward her office door. But she didn't reach it before E.J. could ask another question.

"Did you do something wrong?"

Amy turned back.

"I don't think so."

E.J. nodded.

"That's good."

Amy stepped into the office and opened the familiar Facebook group, the only place she felt comfortable sharing what had just happened.

"Well, the governor's senior advisor sent 8 police officers to make sure I'm not suicidal (which I'm not), so at least now I know they read their emails."

It felt good to have this group to vent with. Amy wasn't sure what she'd do without them, especially on a night like tonight.

The comments would be the difference between being able to sleep that night and lying awake in distress:

"I greatly admire the way you've handled all of this when many of us (myself included) have shrunken into ourselves. Bravo, honestly."

"None of them know the suffering of this industry because they have a paycheck."

"Thanks for always going leaps and bounds to help us."

Despite the love from her colleagues in the group, her sense of humor over the whole situation—the wasted resources, confused officers, and lack of state response—began to sublimate into something else.

Amy had a gut feeling that she'd ignored until her pulse had finally slowed. She sighed and turned off her computer, plunging her home office into darkness.

Opening her phone, Amy dialed Miranda, one of her longtime friends, and someone who had a good deal of knowledge about, well, stuff like this. And to her surprise, Miranda answered.

"Oh my gosh, I am so sorry calling you this late. I thought it'd go to voicemail. Do you mind?"

This was Miranda, though. Always as alert as she was helpful, even this close to midnight.

"Always, Amy."

After a short recap, Amy explained the thought that had crept into her mind.

"I just felt like something didn't add up. I've read my email a hundred times, like, I can send it to you. Maybe it was too much, but—"

Miranda cut her off. If she'd hoped Miranda was going to sate her worry, what she got instead was the total opposite.

"Amy, you need to be careful."

Amy's pulse skyrocketed for the umpteenth time that day.

"Careful of what?"

Miranda sighed.

"I've worked with people who are, and I'm not kidding, minutes away from self-harm. Like, the real deal. Weapons and shit that can hurt me just as bad as them. And hell, that suicide team hasn't shown up one time. I've driven people in my own car to the damn hospital because those squads are nowhere to be found. And that's the norm. There's like, three of those units in the whole county."

"Oh. So what then?"

"I don't mean to scare you, but it seems like it's a message of some kind."

Miranda paused, not sure if she should continue.

"Uh, thanks for saying so."

After hanging up, Amy turned her computer back on, flooding the room with light again. She wasn't going to be getting sleep after a conversation like that, so she might as well get back to work.

It's not easy to sleep on the worst night of your life.

What was impossible to know was that an even worse night would arrive two weeks later.

17
INSIDE BASEBALL

San Diego, CA – February 19th, 2021

For all that had happened at the end of January, the governor's lifting of stay-at-home orders had almost totally been lost in the shuffle. As a matter of fact, it had been announced on the last day of E.J.'s stay at Rady's.

For once, Amy hadn't been madly searching for his livestream, rather, she'd spent that day learning about blood glucose levels. On a different floor at Rady's, though, the Pfizer and Moderna vaccines that held the key to the end of the pandemic were already being distributed to healthcare workers.

While California took care to properly freeze their vials and dole out dosages to demographics that needed it most, it soon would become a mad dash.

If Amy had wanted the vaccine early, she could join those lining up for extra doses at the pharmacy down the street from her house. But there weren't hours to waste by joining in yet another sign of the times.

The CAPE members each appeared on Amy's computer, one by one. They had recently started to blitz anyone and everyone who would listen to them, from assembly members to state senators and public health officials, just as Kevin had taught Amy to do almost five months ago, and still encouraged.

Now, the approach would be a mix of love and anger, because neither had worked on its own. Though, the reply email that Amy had sent in the early hours of January 27th, the morning after the police visit, hadn't hurt.

"Hey, thanks for sending the police to my house. I would have preferred five minutes on your calendar."

This approach had already gotten CAPE a slow trickle of meetings. In a few short days, that trickle snowballed into a flood, and each board member had probably contacted every elected representative with last names "A" to "P" or "Q" by now.

If there hadn't been so many "S" last names, they might have pushed all the way to the Z's.

It was a call every thirty minutes for each of them, back to back to back.

If their message had been at all flawed before, they were now able to recite it like clockwork: cases were falling, the state could be back in orange or yellow tiers within as little as nine weeks, and their industry was desperate for lead times. If they lost this summer, the effects would be felt statewide, and local economies would lose their last chance for recovery.

With the rapid-fire meetings, the whole thing took on a new ease. No longer were Amy or any of her board members nervous around government brass. The experience made them all collectively better at sifting the genuine helpers from the smooth talkers too.

When it came time for a truly impactful meeting, they would be ready. And today would be that meeting, which after more emailing and coordination with legislative staff, would take place with CDPH staff, just before their meeting that afternoon where they would discuss private events for the first time.

As the board members shared hellos and recapped their work that week, with whom they'd met and what they'd accomplished, they couldn't ignore the elephant in the room, and a topic that Amy had hoped to get ahead of before someone had the chance to ask, "Is everything OK?"

The question, which had come while Amy was lost in thought about what she'd say to CDPH and GO-Biz, flooded her with dread. She'd already been asked by friends, neighbors, and others, to whom she'd given the same story.

"I appreciate you asking," she feigned.

She raised her hand to her face, checking for residual pain around a black eye.

"Fender bender this weekend."

"I'm so sorry! That's terrible!"

Amy smiled politely as the others on the call agreed and offered their condolences.

"It's fine. Don't want it to be a distraction. Could have been worse, right?"

The board nodded and returned to the next order of business, most of them not realizing Amy had lied.

Her black eye wasn't from a car accident or a bad fall, two of the many excuses she'd prepared that week for so many, even her own children. The black eye came on the worst night of her life, and one she didn't wish to revisit or recapitulate.

If there had been a moment where Amy could have given up her mission (and no one would have faulted her for doing so), this might have been it. Anyone else who'd made it that far and suffered so many setbacks might as well have decided that was the best choice.

But once her safety had been re-established, Amy was more determined than ever to reach the end of this journey, black eye and all.

If anything, Amy's bruise was a physical manifestation of the injuries she'd suffered since her business had closed, and she only wished politicians could see those scars too.

***

March 12th, 2021

"What. The. Actual. F*CK!!!!"

While "love and anger" was the approach with the state, Amy wasn't afraid to show undiluted anger around those she loved on the Facebook group.

The tier list released that morning was half red and half purple, at long last. Based on early March numbers, the state was finally en route to a loosening of restrictions. But their tier updates only a week prior had been abhorrent, and spurred Amy's explicit post.

"The state just released their 'new guidance' which means you can go to a MLB game but not have a reception. It is COMPLETELY unacceptable."

Hundreds of calls and emails later, some of which had been answered for the first time in months, the Public Health Department had returned to the negotiating table. Moreover, Newsom's office of business and development (GO-Biz), had finally taken them seriously enough to correspond too, at least with phrases like, "We expect to release new guidance for events such as weddings in the coming weeks." And "This past year has been really difficult for so many, including you. But there is a light at the end of the tunnel."

Amy shared, "Their new blueprint says gatherings of no more than three households can gather at a time - EVEN THROUGH TIER 4! This is after we have spent SIX MONTHS sending case studies from other states and asking to operate according to guidelines already approved for restaurants and Hollywood."

If it was all money-driven at the end of the day, rage wasn't going to change their minds. They had to be incentivized and pressured, all at once.

"Hi all, thank you so much for taking the time," Amy said to the administration members on this day's call.

"When we met a few weeks ago, we made it clear how important it was that the private events industry be taken seriously. Private events include 93,000 small businesses in our state, and over three million workers too. Our tax contributions fill state coffers year after year, through tourism, income, and so much more. It's crucial that you give us guidance to move forward, especially with the long lead times we need to serve our clients."

The woman from GO-Biz nodded and replied, "Yes, of course."

"We'd like to know, what are you going to do about it? And when?"

The woman blinked, as if her answers for such a question didn't compute. She seemed to be expecting a presentation and was taken aback when no slides appeared.

"Oh yes, well…"

She pretended to check notes on the table before her, but her stall was easy to see through.

"We were actually wondering what, um, documentation your staff could share with us. We haven't been looped in on some of your meetings, I don't think."

"We have plans and guidance we've submitted. On three or four other occasions, since last June."

"Oh, really?"

The woman looked at another Brady Bunch-esque floating head on her own computer.

"Dr. Gordon, did we–ah yes, you actually did mention this to me. Their guidance?"

One of the CDPH scientists answered, "We have an older version of it. I could check or go through last meeting's notes."

The GO-Biz woman shook her head.

"Why don't you just send it to me, and you can even walk us through it again, while we're all here."

She grinned politely.

Behind the smile, though, was something Amy hadn't sensed in any of these meetings: a legitimate request. It seemed like they needed help.

"Let's start with this. I was able to find wedding guidance on the CDPH site. Right now, based on guidance from, let's see, November thirteenth of last year? Clicking 'Are Weddings Allowed' leads to a limit of three households, including the bride and groom. The fine print further states that weddings can't have a reception at all, beyond the ceremony."

"Sure," the woman answered, "and that's where we were considering starting today. Maybe for tier 4, the yellow tier, we might be able to increase capacity to five households, or something along those lines. Does that sound about right?"

"No."

The call went silent as the woman tensed up.

Months earlier, Amy might have answered more professionally than that. But not today.

"Well then, that's… I guess, why we're all here, right?"

"Yes. We have guidelines that explicitly match what other industries have been permitted to do, some of them now for months. If you want to lose these again, I can promise you, the emails won't stop. We'll come back up there in the wedding gowns and tuxedos and do our march all over again, every day until one of my credit cards gets so bad that they lock me up and throw away the key."

Amy caught one of the CAPE board members hiding a grin on their side of the screen.

The administration members all began to focus intently while the GO-Biz woman smiled and shrugged.

"When you're ready, just, you know, fire away."

***

Sacramento, CA – April 2nd, 2021

FOR IMMEDIATE RELEASE

State Updates Blueprint to Allow Additional Activities with Modifications to Reduce Risk: Updates to gatherings, receptions, conferences, and indoor live events and performances are effective April 15

With vaccination rates increasing and the state's COVID-19 test positivity rate near a record low, the California Department of Public Health (CDPH) today released updates to the state's Blueprint for a Safer Economy reopening framework allowing additional activities to resume with modifications to reduce risk. The updates include gatherings, private events or meetings such as receptions or conferences, and indoor seated live events and performances. These updates take effect April 15. California's framework for loosening and tightening restrictions is governed by the level of COVID-19 spread.

"As we continue to expand vaccine distribution, California is poised for a safe and equitable recovery," said GO-Biz representative Dee Dee Myers. "We will continue to work with businesses, arts organizations, community groups and others to open carefully, with health and safety top of mind, so that we never have to go backwards."

18

WIPE AWAY THE TIERS

Downtown San Diego – June 15th, 2021

The Quartyard, located in the heart of downtown San Diego, was one of Amy's favorite downtown venues.

When one thinks of a downtown venue, enclosed spaces top the list: clubs, penthouses, and strictly permitted public parks among them. But the Quartyard was different: at the corner of Market and 13th, the venue had an enclosure with a stage and the backdrop of beautiful San Diego on all sides.

And tonight truly would be beautiful.

While "June gloom" was just as prevalent in San Diego as it was in Los Angeles, that gloom had stayed at home this afternoon. Judging by the traffic getting to the Quartyard, no one else was at home. Tonight was a citywide opportunity for celebration.

One year and three months had passed since Amy's call with Paula, almost to the day. The Beer Festival, the CROSS'd fest… it all seemed like a lifetime ago. But March 2020 was still shockingly recent in the grand scheme of things.

Amy didn't miss the challenge of parking downtown, which had returned too. But it wasn't long before she'd found a parallel spot and unloaded the family.

QUARTYARDSD-DOT-COM, the Scrabble-style sign out front read, with more text below: SAVE OUR STAGE. Quartyard had almost disappeared with First Comes Love, despite its outdoor advantages. The venue had even been stripped of its ability to host pet gatherings, which was a favorite for its neighbors that lacked serviceable dog parks downtown.

Protestors holding signs and banners, even megaphones, had gathered in front of the chain link fences that connected Quartyard to the sidewalk.

Amy tried to stay focused on keeping Ariana or E.J. from stumbling off the sidewalk, as kids always seem to be doing on busy city streets, though she couldn't help but glance over to read one or two of the signs.

"SAN DIEGO CITIZENS SAY FLETCHER DESERVES NO AWARD."

Amy had expected there would be something like this, and was glad that the San Diego Event Coalition, led by Ellen, had done such good work with security. The guards let her through the gates as soon as they recognized the family.

For all that Amy had been through, and despite Fletcher's lone "no" vote almost exactly a year prior, Amy didn't envy his position, nor did she envy his new promotion to chair of the board, replacing Greg Cox. That was the dichotomy of COVID decision making at any level or company: somebody would always be pissed. And sometimes too, both sides would be.

Inside the walls of Quartyard, where hundreds had gathered from all corners of the event industry, Amy immediately recognized other familiar signs of protest, the very boards and posters that CAPE and SDEC had protested with, now lying at many of the now-occupied tables.

For once, "SAVE SMALL BUSINESSES, SUPPORT EVENT WORKERS" didn't send pangs of stress through her veins. The light at the end of the tunnel was here, and quite literally, as the setting sun warmed the venue, and would undoubtedly create a gorgeous sunset behind the Mark Skyscraper in a half hour or so.

Almost immediately, Ariana and E.J. had left Amy's side, already sprinting toward the stage where a deejay played music that they started to dance to. They gyrated about with the childhood energy that they'd been so forced to bottle up these past months.

A dance group snapped photos at the photo booth to Amy's left, where a KUSI reporting team set up a little further behind them. Hopefully they would cover the event more so than the protests, but at this point, it wasn't Amy's fight. At least, not alone.

Tonight, Amy could celebrate. And it felt good.

Maybe they hadn't accomplished everything they set out to do when they wanted to accomplish it, but in the end, CAPE had forced their cause at the highest levels, and had gained the very seat at the table they'd so desired. Had that final push not happened when the tiers first debuted, Amy wasn't sure they'd be here today, or that she could have held on any longer.

The road to recovery still wasn't perfect, especially when it came to her credit, but she hadn't lost the Summer of 2021. Weddings were trickling back, and soon might boom again.

What a bizarre journey it had all been. And what a fitting end to it all, an event in which county and city government members were just as numerous as industry colleagues. Now, Amy wasn't the only one with a connection at the city or county level, nor was Ellen. It was the whole industry who could act with and alongside the Jim Desmonds, Gary Johnstons, and Nathan Fletchers.

If their livelihoods ever were threatened again, either for COVID reasons or something else entirely, they wouldn't be caught flatfooted. CAPE membership was brewing and would quickly make for a third successful entrepreneurial effort after First Comes Love and the Best Coast Beer Festival, the latter of which would also get one last hurrah in the months to come.

Maybe CAPE wouldn't keep up at the pace it had in 2020 and the start of 2021, but if the event professionals were able to go back to normal life again, that would be as much a success as any. CAPE would always be there, should they need to band together again and take their fight to the county, state, or even Washington, D.C. (If it was up to the couple hundred active members of the Facebook group, Amy would have already been elected president. In their eyes, basic community politicking was more than enough of a qualifier.)

Relishing a bittersweet end to a life in politics only grew sweeter with the arrival of Supervisor Fletcher and his wife, which was obvious due to the commotion from the protest outside, riled up like a hornet's nest.

Amy spent her drink ticket and stepped into a throng of friends, reconnecting with everyone from the CAPE board to Gary Johnston. She tried to focus on the video board, which recapped multiple protests and empty venue day, with an occasional glance toward the entryway. Ellen did her due diligence to welcome Nathan and pull him as far away from the chanting as possible.

With a slight increase of volume from the deejay, the protests were drowned out enough for the event to commence. And by the time the Brickhouse dance team had taken the stage, they were underway.

Ellen spoke first. Her story, and path to leading SDEC was similar to Amy's.

"I was sitting in Utah, looking at layers on the earth on all sides, and feeling sorry for myself. I realized, community events do not have a voice, and we are being left out of all of the conversations…. We used word-of-mouth and started to grow. We used every community and story to fight for our livelihood, our families, and for the right to be seen and heard."

Amy nodded in agreement, as did those standing around her, in between the occasional glance toward the Padres' away game, televised just above the bar.

Ellen finished, "We got a ton of no's and 'we can't help you's, but we're used to that in the event industry, and I always say, 'A no is a "maybe" on the way to a yes.'"

The crowd laughed warmly. After announcing the coalition's official 501(c)(6) status, Ellen cheered, "Today, for the San Diego event community, this is our first day of being officially open!"

Ellen's second awardee of a trio was Gary, who needed no introduction, but she gave him a great one anyway.

"Gary spent hours going through and helping us create the guidelines for community events. At the same time, he helped us find ways for some of our members to hold our events by using other guidance…. He took the time to care and listen. He listened to our fears, our concerns, our deepest worries that would wake us up in the middle of the night…. He told us to never stop fighting and to keep going when we felt like we had lost the battle over and over and over."

Applause welcomed Gary to the podium. He was his usual self and matched his job description: resilient. Even the protests still at the perimeter quieted when he took the microphone.

"Welcome back," he roared, to cheers from the crowd.

"Welcome back!"

After a few brief thank you's and a recap of his first experiences in the job, especially the aspects that felt like building an airplane in flight without a pilot's license, Gary clenched his jaw and flared his nostrils.

"Quite frankly, we all know there are a bunch of you who aren't here, because your businesses didn't survive."

He pointed, not at anything in particular, but in the military way that a superior might encourage their peers.

"It's not missed on us the sacrifices you made with respect to your business, your families, your savings…. You are back."

The crowd cheered one more time, before the protests returned to full force as Sup. Fletcher took the stage to accept the third and final award, accompanied by a short speech.

It was hard to hear what Nathan was saying, but Amy did ironically make out the phrase, "I wish we could've done more sooner."

The supervisor would be nice enough to take photos and chat with fellow San Diegans before using a fire exit to make his escape, only moments before the mob had realized they'd been misdirected and chased his SUV down Market Street as it sped away.

Amy grinned ear to ear as she was able to shake hands with Gary, in person at long last.

"Amy, hey!"

"Thanks Gary, for everything."

"Just following that county motto."

"What's that?"

For all of Amy's work with the county, she didn't know that answer.

"The noblest motive is the public good."

"That's a good one."

For all the feelings, worries, and relief that the night had brought, there was still one more thing on Amy's to do list, and it was what brought the biggest smile to her face.

She helped E.J. and Ariana back up to the stage and let them go nuts as they had upon arrival, as the deejay turned up the music again.

Amy cheered them on and pulled out her phone to video, but soon pocketed it. Raising her arms and smiling ear to ear, Amy joined her children in their dance. And the past was put to rest.

***

San Diego, CA – June 22nd, 2021

We don't realize when we're doing a routine for the last time, and that was the case for Amy as she half-mindedly opened SD Events group.

Today wasn't a list of asks, nor a lengthy petition. It wasn't even a casual remark.

It was just ten words.

"Need wedding assistants. If anyone is interested, please email me."

19
HINDSIGHT 2021

Sacramento, CA – July 29th, 2021

For all the time Gavin Newsom spent speaking, there were very few people who knew he was dyslexic. It wasn't something he wore as a badge of pride, nor was it something he let define him.

His dyslexia wasn't just a childhood passing, as it is for the lucky majority of those who can receive treatment. Rather Gavin's dyslexia still influenced him. Earlier in his life, he may not have readily embraced the daily, then weekly, COVID pressers he'd hosted. He certainly would not have tolerated an hour-long Q&A session with opinion editors from the *Sacramento Bee* and others, as he would today.

Today, Gavin didn't have a set of notes to memorize, or an hour to fill airwaves with his own prepared words. He was at the mercy of the press. And they smelled blood in the water, now that a recall effort had grown from within his own state.

What the press had gotten wrong about Gavin in his time in public office infuriated him to no end. Whether it was "MeBored" or simple requests of data that got lost in the shuffle, the press always took their chance to pounce when he showed any weakness. Many times, the lack of correspondence wasn't done for bad reasons either, just staff changes at the worst possible moments.

Gavin didn't ask for the world when it came to fair coverage. No person with so much scrutiny could expect the impossible. What he did ask for was an ounce of respect for his transparency, especially in an age when politicians could very easily opt to do otherwise. Those that did even seemed to escape scrutiny as some kind of twisted reward for their dishonesty.

In that vein, transparency hadn't saved his administration from the growing threat of recall, and whether it was a trip to downtown San Francisco to help clean homeless encampments or his rapid loosening of COVID restrictions, the recall polls only showed more concerning results with each passing week.

Gavin wasn't afraid that he'd ever lose the majority needed to win the day, but the challenge still felt accessory to what he still hoped to accomplish as governor. After all the work, and a leadership performance that far outstripped most other governors and even world leaders, Gavin faced a recall.

Not Abbott, not Cuomo, and not Desantis, but Gavin and Gavin alone.

Part of his PR campaign efforts included interviews like this one, and interviews that were atypical for plenty of those aforementioned governors. Leaning back in a dress shirt at his desk, he forced a smile as soon as the interview video began recording.

Bright sunlight peeked through the window to his right as he tried to identify which of the Bee's editors would ask questions that fairly evaluated his performance, rather than dip into "gotcha" journalism.

It wasn't war just yet. Once he was able to traverse the rocky ground of the still-reverberating French Laundry incident, the coast would be clear. With the interview posted in unedited form, Gavin looked forward to having his words wholly included, rather than edited into bite-sized half-truths.

"Governor, thank you so, so much for joining us."

The executive editor of the *Sacramento Bee* opened the group video call, right after the off-camera pleasantries had resolved.

Gavin leaned back in his chair, just right of center frame. To his left, the American flag and the flag of California draped together. To his right, a series of shelves sported a house plant and a series of carefully selected books, just as any video interviewee had learned to do over the past year.

While a good politician has a smile at the ready, a great politician can maintain a smile even when they'd rather do otherwise. Today would be a battle to be great, and in the face of the worst that the press had to throw at him.

For now, Gavin was able to muster the smile that you might show to a disliked coworker as you cross paths in the break room.

The editor continued, "I wanted to kick things off by asking you to tell us what you think is at stake in this recall."

Maybe there would be curveballs for which he was unprepared, but at least the first question was a fastball right over the plate. Rattling off the standard talking points put him at ease as the minutes began to tick off the clock.

Hijacked recall process…

Right-wing media…

Newt Gingrich…

The more talking points he could summon, the fewer curveballs these pitchers might have time to throw. Newsom didn't fear Faulconer, Elder, or any of the other candidates, but he did fear what the recall did to the appearance of his first thirty months on the job. Good work takes time, and the recall struck at a moment when so many of his administration's efforts were still getting their feet under them.

"It's interesting to me, it's always curious, how few people actually read the petition that was signed," Gavin continued, elaborating further than he had during any of the rallies against the effort. He tugged at his shirt collar, almost like a cartoon character trying to let some heat escape their neckline.

"Including, respectfully, members of the media."

He opened his hands in a shrug, and truly smiled for the first time in the interview. Hopefully the vultures wouldn't take too much offense to a little jab, or Gavin's equating them to "pundits" half a sentence later.

"I think the pandemic created conditions, some more situational, some more existential as the nation was grappling with approaches, no playbook. We all moved, every state, every state moved in some way, shape, or form to physical distancing, social distancing…. It created an environment where there was cause and effect, and a lot of raw emotion across the spectrum, across the country, from both political parties."

The next two questions, one from the *Modesto Bee* and the other from the *San Luis Obispo Tribune*, were change-ups at best: the first related to the water wars raging in the central valley, the latter to energy policy. With a sleek sprint through negotiations, megawatts, and gigawatts, the interview was now a quarter of the way over.

Next up was the *Fresno Bee*, which had the first curveball at the ready. The tricky thing about curveball questions is how simple they sound. Any journalist can nitpick a statistic from a campaign speech and find an inefficiency with hindsight on their side. Answering those questions was a lose/lose by Gavin's estimation. Either you sound like a liar, or worse, you appear unfit to serve.

"When you campaigned for governor, you said you'd oversee construction of 3.5 million homes by 2025. So far, on your governorship, if my research is right, less than 100,000 homes annually have been built…. What specifically are you doing to increase housing production today? And why should a young couple starting out, or a young family looking to put down roots, believe you can make a difference for them?"

The distaste on Newsom's face was apparent.

"I say this with respect, Ted. The facts…need some reconsideration."

Marcos Bretón would complain in the article attached to the interview, "The governor…challenged the premise of more than one question posed to him."

What was so out-of-bounds about seeking fair questioning? In what cruel world were politicians supposed to treat every question as legitimate when the premise of the inquiry was taken out of context?

It was attention to detail that got California through this pandemic, until it came time to sell papers, apparently. It was another writer at the Bee who would follow in those footsteps, not citing nitpicked data, but instead opting to cite no data at all.

She asked, in essence, why homelessness was worsening. And Gavin leaned in.

He usually tried not to do that, since his webcam was situated above him, and leaning back gave him the best appearance. But there was no avoiding it. He was ready to attack this one head-on.

"Well, we also got 42,000 people off the streets last year," he retorted.

The interview went silent. The caption on the video momentarily read, BLANK AUDIO.

Those sorts of pauses always worked for dramatic effect. They worked better in person, because the interviewee would suddenly have the tables turned on them. Here, his accusers could hide behind the visual safety of their Brady Bunch cells.

The pause, which only lasted a few seconds, yet felt no less than a minute long, was broken by Gavin's explanation of Project Room Key, one of the more successful initiatives to rehabilitate the homeless with faster and more effective results. That put him back in control of the interview, and at ease, allowing him to burn more clock, like a run-heavy football offense with a narrow fourth-quarter lead.

But as Army football goes, once you've played out enough zones, tosses, and keepers, the defense realizes there's no passing game to defend, and they try to stuff you at the line.

As Gavin entered the fourth or fifth minute of his answer to the homelessness question, he raised his voice, shaking his head.

"I am just winding up. I am really looking forward to the application, implementation, and a $1.1 billion budget on top of that," as he pointed and slapped both hands against his desk, "to clean up the damn streets and to deal with these encampments."

He continued, now pointing not into camera, but at the screen where his questioners all blankly stared from their offices scattered around the northern half of the state.

"And I've been personally doing that, dozens of times. Not just with all your fancy reporters, Sophia, God bless, but with folks when the cameras aren't there. I've been out there cleaning the damn streets from Fresno, Tad," as he pointed to another corner of his screen, "to down there in Stockton, and every part of the state."

After a few grievances about mayors not implementing encampment budgetary measures in between table slaps and a few more uses of the D-word, Gavin careened back into his chair, slanted to the side. He might have looked relaxed or relieved to have let loose in that moment, were it not for the finger pressed to his lips.

If this sixty-minute interview were that football game, the third quarter was nearly flawless, as Gavin adeptly navigated questions on climate change and forest fire management between minutes thirty and forty-five.

But then came the questions on crime and another question about the disappearing California dream. The former got Gavin angry thinking about how helpless he was to intervene, with many of the judges and district attorneys acting of their own accord, and that anger set the stage for the final questions.

At that moment, showing some skin felt good. Here in a long-form interview that the governor knew wouldn't be heavily edited, he could make his case against the recall. He could show his constituents where he was truly working on their behalf and attempt to drag opinion writers in the right direction.

"You guys, forgive me. I know I've been a little pointed today," he admitted.

"But I've been taking a lot from," he paused, considering rewording, but then continued with, "you folks for a lot of months. So it's nice to be able to express myself too."

The flurry of those final few minutes, even after the apology, was what would make headlines in the days to come.

"We're number one in job creation... eat your heart out, Texas and Florida.... I know you're gonna Politifact this, and you're gonna find something and go run with it, and I'll look forward to seeing what I screwed up. It's all off the top of my damn head.... Hell, I did a six-billion-dollar signing ceremony in Nunes's back damn district on a bill he opposed.... I'm proud of the fact that our agriculture, our fishing, and our logging industry is bigger than the next five states combined! That's California!"

And for the grand finale, "It'd be damn nice if our homegrown teams started focusing on what's right. Everyone outside the state is bitching about this state because of our success, and I'm proud of it."

Gavin had finally gotten the French Laundry off the airwaves, because his rivals and allies both would take these sound bites and run much further with them.

So be it.

He'd held back for years, wanting to tell the media how he felt about their coverage, and it was finally time they were dealt the honesty they so desperately wished to peddle.

It was time to turn the tides on the recall, which he desired to win and win convincingly.

After that, the future was bright.

ACKNOWLEDGEMENTS

This book is full of brave people, and not just those who met the moment of COVID, but also those who spoke with me about their experiences.

Amy, thank you for trusting me with your story, and for taking the time out of your busy schedule rebuilding First Comes Love to tell that story.

In early 2021, when we started this journey, I thought this might be a documentary. Then, you were nice enough to take more time to craft a book proposal with me. After months in consideration, that proposal finally got its chance, and with even more interviews, you got us to the finish line.

Thank you, Kevin, for taking time to not only interview with me, but also for providing such detailed information throughout the process. Thank you, Lisa, for coordinating.

Thank you, Gary, for choosing to make your story known, and for being the hero that San Diego, and any average person in the entire state of California, needed but didn't deserve.

Additionally, I'd like to mention that Gary's team's impeccable after-action report on COVID in San Diego can be found at <https://www.readysandiego.org/content/dam/oesready/en/aar/County_of_San_Diego_COVID19_AAR_and_Response_Documents_Final_20230310.pdf>.

Thank you, Sage, for your interview and continued feedback. I think you were one of the first I interviewed, and I can't thank you enough for your work on behalf of photographers everywhere.

Thank you, Megan Porth and YourContractShop.com, and the Scottsdale HUUB grants program.

A big thanks to Kimberly Peticolas and the Rudy Agency for securing the two-book deal that led to both my literary debut and this return to the medium.

Thank you, Lana, Laura, and to all my Moving Picture Institute fellows for guiding the very earliest stages of this story, back in its documentary stage.

Thank you, Deacon Paul, for your spiritual guidance and liturgical wizardry.

Thank you, Thomas Marshall, for sharing your MFA-caliber writer's insight with me.

Finally, I'd like to thank the friends and family who made the sacrifice to join our wedding. We love you.

There are many public figures who were featured here to the most accurate of my abilities. Thanks to quick work by Histria Books, I'm happy to have been able to release this book in a timely manner. So if you're wondering, "where are they now?" turn on the news and find out.

REFERENCES

(2020, March 19 and November 16). CA Governor. Facebook. Retrieved December 1, 2022, from <https://www.facebook.com/CAgovernor>.

(2020, June 23). June 23 County Agenda. San Diego County Board of Supervisors. Retrieved January 1, 2023, from <https://content.govdelivery.com/attachments/CASAND/2020/06/17/file_attacHments/1476165/062320%20Regular_Agenda.pdf>.

Breton, M. (2021, September 21). "News on the Blueprint for a Safer Economy." *Sacramento Bee*. Retrieved December 15, 2022, from <https://www.sacbee.com/article253268593.html>.

CDPH (n.d.). COVID-19 Monitoring Overview. California Dept. of Public Health. Retrieved January 1, 2023, from <https://www.cdph.ca.gov/Programs/CID/DCDC/Pages/COVID-19/COVID19CountyMonitoringOverview.aspx>.

CDPH (n.d.). News on the Blueprint for a Safer Economy. California Dept. of Public Health. Retrieved December 15, 2022, from <https://www.cdph.ca.gov/Programs/CID/DCDC/Pages/COVID-19/News-on-the-Blueprint-for-a-Safer-Economy.aspx>.

Flamm, Caleb. "George Santayana (1863—1952)." Internet Encyclopedia of Philosophy.

Fletcher, N. (2013, May 4). Nathan Fletcher Post. Facebook. Retrieved December 15, 2022, from <https://www.facebook.com/nathan.fletcher/posts/pfbid0LnT6N6fpFMEbJ6iJEJ5k4XXSBcbV6UANebTAo1RGsqarvd1jRBuxFwXX6xaJpgUpl>.

Lin, R. G., II (2020, June 22). "Social gatherings help fuel rising coronavirus spread in parts of California." *Los Angeles Times*. Retrieved December 1, 2022, from <https://www.latimes.com/california/story/2020-06-22/social-gatherings-coronavirus-spread-california>.

Newsom, Gavin, and Lisa Dickey. *Citizenville: How to Take the Town Square Digital and Reinvent Government*. Penguin Books, 2014.

"SB-2005." California Senate (1993-1994) - Open States, https://open-states.org/ca/ bills/19931994/SB2005/.

AUTHOR BIO

Rob is the author of *Power to the Players* (2023) and the sci-fi/action novel, *Backfill*. He's also a writer and director of feature films, including *The Last Whistle* (2019) and *Walkout: Change within the World's Largest Company* (2024). Rob and his wife Kate remain happily married and have since welcomed a labradoodle into their family.

SUBJECT BIO

Amy da Silva resides in San Diego with her children. First Comes Love had its best year ever in 2022 and continues to succeed, so much so that Amy was finally able to get her dream Tesla.

HISTRIA
BOOKS

GAUDIUM

GAUDIUM PUBLISHING
BOOKS TO CHALLENGE AND ENLIGHTEN

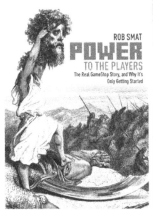

ROB SMAT

POWER
TO THE PLAYERS
The Real GameStop Story, and Why It's
Only Getting Started

OLIVIA GOODREAU

BUT SHE LOOKS FINE

FROM ILLNESS TO ACTIVISM

THE SILVER BULLET SOLUTION
IS IT TIME TO END THE WAR ON DRUGS?

JAMES E. GIERACH

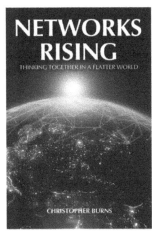

NETWORKS RISING
THINKING TOGETHER IN A FLATTER WORLD

CHRISTOPHER BURNS

MACRON •
Unveiled
THE PROTOTYPE FOR A NEW GENERATION OF WORLD LEADERS
ALAIN LEFEBVRE

A Tale of Two Villains
THEME AND SYMBOLISM IN
Dracula and the Harry Potter Saga

Calvin Cherry

FOR THESE AND OTHER GREAT BOOKS VISIT
HISTRIABOOKS.COM